Life's New Dawn

Rev. Paul Kumar

Bloomington, IN Milton Keynes, UK

authorHOUSE™

AuthorHouse™
1663 Liberty Drive, Suite 200
Bloomington, IN 47403
www.authorhouse.com
Phone: 1-800-839-8640

AuthorHouse™ UK Ltd.
500 Avebury Boulevard
Central Milton Keynes, MK9 2BE
www.authorhouse.co.uk
Phone: 08001974150

First published by AuthorHouse 4/11/2006

ISBN: 1-4259-2419-0 (sc)
ISBN: 1-4259-2418-2 (dj)

Library of Congress Control Number: 2006902847

Printed in the United States of America
Bloomington, Indiana

This book is printed on acid-free paper.

DEDICATED TO

This love of mine, my beloved, my wife,
my inspiration, my instructor, my guide,
my counsel, my cheer, my encouragement,
my lighthouse through dark moments,
my support and strength through frailty,
my wisdom when in doubt and fear.
Summing it all up, unlike any other,
MY WIFE—HEAVEN SENT HER TO ME!

PAUL KUMAR

ACKNOWLEDGMENTS

A heart of gratitude to:

My son Victor, who came into our world as a gift from God, now with God smiling favorably upon his own family....

My daughter Monisha, a jewel as described by her namewith a heart full of caring for others with Love.

Her birth was a miracle of her own, along with her parents'. She is today a mother loving her two children.

My daughter Sabrina stepped upon U.S. soil with life to commemorate the bicentennial year 1976. She is very determined to forge her way in life, on her own, with God's watchful eyes upon her.

The backup team that makes the family circle:

Jenny—A good wife and mother to Kaylee and Gavin; the lifeline, as completed by her husband, Victor.

Jason—A man of goodwill and compassion for everyone around. He is a loving father to son Austin and daughter Avery, and devoted to his wife Monisha.

To two dedicated, unfailing servants of Christ:

Rev. and Mrs. Winston Harmon, the pastor and wife who obeyed God's direction to see through this heart of mine to help me proclaim the Gospel of Jesus Christ to everyone, and granted me a license to preach in their ministry, which is a prerequisite of man! My resolve is, as the apostle Paul wrote to young Timothy, "Fight for God, hold tightly to the eternal Life which God has given you, and which you have confessed with such a ringing confession, before many witnesses."
1 Timothy 6:12

It is truly gratifying to remember the touch of human caring with expertise in publishing to the staff and special teams at Author House, Bloomington Indiana.

Some names stand and deserve mention:
- David Pruett, Author House Sales Representative, for guidance and spiritual support along the way.
- Jennifer Brandt, for her purpose and vision of publication and in serving as the Design Consultant for Author House.
- Lori Fender, Author House Creative Department, for her expertise in personalized printing that makes the title well appealing to each page and chapter of its content. Much in awe and gratitude to the excellence in the art work in capturing the "New Dawn "in its glory and grandeur.

Grateful for the Promotion team in helping spreading the good news of real life experiences captured in "Life's New Dawn".

"I thank my God upon every
remembrance of you ...Philippians 1:3

Rev. Paul Kumar

INTRODUCTION

THE AWAKENING INTO LIFE'S NEW DAWN

IN EVERY PERSON'S LIFE there come many others who become very close to affecting and changing our course in life powerfully. This story is about two people who fell in love in the most unusual circumstances, totally diverse in every way in their own lifestyles. Consider the setting with the backdrop of India, oceans away from the hot, sultry, dusty roads, with burning heat rising as steam and people from all walks of life scurry, often aimlessly, just to make a day of living worthwhile! A great blend of the populace is from a big city such as Madras, which recently changed its name to Chennai, in South India. These two lives had never crossed paths before, for strange reasons. One was a poor Christian, a son born and raised as a teacher's only child. The other was a very pretty young woman of twenty-three years, a twin amid three brothers and wealthy parents. Raised in the Hindu faith, she was very traditional and strictly observed that faith. To add to that, her wealth was notable, with bungalows fenced and gated, with servants to attend (butlers, maids), and with cars to be driven. Madras, now Chennai, is a very bustling seaport humming with trade and business. The landscape, with beautiful sandy beaches stretching for miles, is dotted with fisherman busy bringing to shore fresh fish and shrimp, and there is a marketplace on the seashore itself! Whitewashed bungalows spotlight the rich, and side by side live the poor by the roadside in makeshift boxes as their homes! There are mud huts with thatched leaves for roofs, busy streets, highways with cows (the sacred animal of worship) amid the Hindu population, crisscrossing amid traffic. The cars and buses stop out of respect for those cows, allowing them to cross the road at their own pace! The rich never cared to look beneath the balconies at their surroundings; at life's gray, and the black of hunger, sickness, poverty, and even death on the curbside. In spite of all the darkness of a black night, God was faithful each morning with the break of dawn and the golden sunrises, and in the evening with the hues of orange sunsets, when none of us took the time to stop and marvel at the wonder of God's creation.

With so much uncertainty in their lives, Paul Kumar and Menuka Guha (affectionately called Minnie) bumped into each other in a unique way in a store and fell in LOVE!

LOVE is not always a clear pathway; it has it's hedges lined with thorns when emotions and desires confront disappointments, cruel words, and actions even from within the family, whom we often trust to say they love us, guaranteed! As this story unfolds, it truly has God as the heavenly creator of heaven and earth, and all of His people on earth. He is also the eternal artist, who paints our very lives in rich hues of dark and bright colors, weaving them to form in Paul and Minnie a living testimony to all His plans.

The plans that brought about *Life's New Dawn* into their lives, the life in us, once seemed an impossible dream that became reality in a land called AMERICA! One of our founding fathers spoke so well of what we so proudly uphold in our hearts today: "MY GOD, HOW LITTLE DO MY COUNTRYMEN KNOW WHAT PRECIOUS BLESSINGS THEY ARE IN POSSESSION OF, WHICH NO OTHER PEOPLE ON EARTH ENJOY."

We now understand firsthand that very truth through the ages, from one of the founding fathers of this great nation, shaping the

Rev. Paul Kumar

American dream that continues today and making AMERICA the beautiful from sea to shining sea, where God's blessings pour down for all people. People like us: Paul and Minnie.

LIFE'S NEW DAWN

OUT FARAWAY IN THE LAND OF INDIA, across many oceans, as mystic as ancient history bringing forth life and images, centuries ago powerful emperors like Alexander the Great, Moghul kings, and emperors ran down many a civilization for greed and power! Kings and queens reigned in splendor, where love and romance still blossomed; so much so today that in the land of India, those wars and conflicts still symbolize the power and wealth of that era. There are many landmarks all over India that reveal the past centuries, and the masterpieces in the architecture and the building of grand palaces and monuments, that still stand proud in honor of their very own dreamers who made it happen. One such monument is purely for the extraordinary love of the emperor Shah Jehan, who dedicated it to his wife, Noor Jehan, who died before him. In an act of such deep love as a memorial stands the beautiful, mighty work of art in marble in the city of Agra, close to New Delhi, India's capital city.

The Taj Mahal is world famous and well known, as thousands travel from near and far to behold the stunning edifice in pure marble, a work so perfect made by artisans who worked tirelessly for the emperor Shah Jehan, unlike today with modern tools and building technologies in place. On a cool north Indian evening, one can walk through the gardens lined with fountains dancing. They cast a spell, causing you to fall in love with the person next to you, and everything around you. This beautiful creation of art in marble was, after all, made to pronounce to the emperor's wife the love and the grief that would be forever! This dedication as a memorial to her was to tell the whole world, as it stands even today, of the beauty of her eyes, the true love between them; she as fresh as a rose with her beauty lingering in his eyes; the fragrance of her being, a sweet perfume; her total dedication for her emperor—her love! On a moonlit night, the surroundings become more alive, as the flawless marble stirs even the coldest heart to poetic words and songs of this the memory of one heart for the life of one who was a wife and who loved leaving many spellbound. Still today the moon and a moonlit night beckons us to caress LOVE in its finest form, as a rose with fresh dewdrops on every petal, with a stirring fragrance, reminds us of peace, tranquility, and our hearts to be still, to REMEMBER. What would dawn be like equally against the backdrop a fiery golden sky, with the sun positioned high above this tall-rising building in marble, amid the streams and fountains, and the hush of silence leaving anyone, a tourist, a visitor, spellbound? If I stood there at sunrise one morning, before this grand memorial to a queen, I too could forget my tossed-about heart riding on the crest of the waves of my emotions that remind me of India; it's intricate fabric of many faiths and deep-seated cultures amid the modern world of today, customs that often contradict today's lifestyles of modern India, blended in with the old! It would be sad to compare the present to the grand times in centuries past, when these kings, emperors, rulers, and the Moghul kings in Indian history overran towns, villages, and cities, destroying land, cattle, crops, and people in their desire for wealth and riches, plundering the land as in the tradition of war since time began! Well, I am to begin once again at yet another time in war ... 1941-1944.

In each life, with the joy that comes in the morning—yes, *Life's New Dawn* begins, and in my life, it began during the harsh reality of 1941, a time when the world was in conflict, trying to gain power

Rev. Paul Kumar

and to rule accordingly. With dark gray skies dotted with numerous warplanes, the sound and drones of the planes dropping bombs over a city darkened by blackouts, this was the place where I was born: Madras, now known as Chennai, a thriving busy harbor. This seaport on the east coast of India, at the southern tip, was the point of attack by the Japanese. The continuous rain of bombs dropped by speeding planes caused big splashes in the harbor, where merchant ships were anchored, exposed as they lay open to death and destruction. On land the loud, deafening explosions of the bombs, with high-rising fiery flames that spread throughout the city of Madras, left behind death, and destruction of property. Thousands fled from the city to nearby towns and villages, fleeing from danger and harm. Some, like my brave mother, were determined and married a veteran war correspondent, writer, and journalist. She stayed, praying, for she was to have her first baby anytime soon. Hello! It was my time, to enter into this world, tiny, undernourished, brown in complexion. July 23, 1941, a true red-letter day, for it did not matter if bombs were flying and the war was raging. *Life's New Dawn* was there for a sweet, faithful Christian mother, wife, teacher—a lady of will! As for me, I was placed in a makeshift cradle with the melody of soothing hymns such as "Rock of Ages" sung softly as the cradle rocked.

My mother was a virtuous Christian woman. In this pandemonium of war, *Life's New Dawn* came with God smiling at the birth of her baby. Stop! Where is the father of this baby-to-be to share the joys of a new life? After all, new life is a part of God's unique plan of creation and human life! Well, sad as it was, my father, the prominent writer, journalist, and war correspondent—the lawful husband—was nowhere close by. There was a cruel twist as early as then to this beautiful event of *Life's New Dawn*. My father had already set his mind to use the war and its pangs of uncertainty to aid his career, seeking a change in his life, desiring a new woman, a wife again, leaving my mother and I destitute. The war provided my father a good smokescreen to advance further into his adulterous desires. So little to say of what should have been the pride of his wife, of her husband, and of me, in father—a man to look up to! Pursuing journalism, maybe later in life, could have been one of my goals? Like father like son? It never was that way, sadly, for it was my devoted mother, a proud educator in English in an outstanding English school in Madras, who gave her life for her teaching profession

The baby ... wow! What is his name? Did they not christen the baby? Nothing would escape the resolute will and thinking of my mother! The firstborn remained the only child, with no brothers or sisters to claim. I was named Paul. In her unwavering faith, she must have been reminded of the apostle Paul in the Bible, of his hardships, his trials, his shipwrecks and imprisonments that always led him to proudly call upon Christ, and who sought Christ's leadership in his life. With the hard truth of her husband, my dad, not coming back to us as a family, she vowed to do it from that moment on: raise me up to the best of her strengths, physically, emotionally, and spiritually, by far.

So began my life. Mother was faithful, trusted Christ first, and read her Bible, looking for comfort, solace, and peace from the scriptures and wisdom from God to manage with a small salary of thirty-five dollars. a month. As a good teacher she would often say without any wavering in her voice, as I grew up through the years, the assurance in her heart: "GOD WILL PROVIDE."

Upon reflection today, as her son, indebted to her with profound gratitude, I compare to her myself, a mature adult, married with three of my own children, who with their families brought forth the joys of being a grandparent. There is that confirmation for every parent: "Train up a child in the way he should go, and when he is old, he will not depart from it" (Proverbs 22:6). They were the powerful bricks that formed the foundation of my life, early on, and to that mother I am much indebted and owe gratitude, as today she is in the place she longed for, in the presence of her Savior, creator, and friend Jesus Christ. My mother never remarried, for she accepted the harshness of her husband, who walked away from those very sacred vows he once made and who spoke in the midst of witnesses, "For rich or for poor, in sickness or in health, till death do you part. Now in God's sight, you

Rev. Paul Kumar

two are as one, husband and wife." Those promises melted like vapor within the dark clouds of deception in the heart of her husband, my father! Raising me was not easy, as I was told often when my mother would speak of my tiny weak infant frame. I was often malnourished, had bronchitis. and could not be given a bath in the tub but simply wiped with a warm towel instead, also known as a sponge bath, till the age of six or seven years, for fear of any chest colds and complications. A gigantic task was charted for her years of raising me up all alone with no one's help; she was a lady four feet eight inches tall, approximately ninety pounds in her short frame, with jet-black hair that took long to gray, and two powerful small eyes of black that observed everything and more!

She was confident and never seemed lost; her face lit up when the name of Christ was spoken, and she truly knew Jesus Christ as her savior. She truly practiced her faith. "By humility and the fear of the Lord are riches and honor and life" (Proverbs 22:4). She had struggles all her life, but still through her resolve I was placed in an English school at the age of two and graduated from high school at the age of fifteen. Discipline in English schools in India is equivalent to that in our private schools here in the U.S. Somehow unable at that age to understand the pains and struggles of life, I still grew up to be a well-mannered young man with a good educational foundation in the English language. Unlike elsewhere in the world, in those years, as early as 1956, India did not offer scholarships to colleges based on merit and grades. Colleges were and still are, higher-learning institutions where you pay and make your way to further your education. Our home lacked such resources, and I had no opportunities to walk the halls of college for higher learning!

The time was at hand for mother and I to make some life-changing decisions. One of those thoughts that came to my mind was to join the Indian armed forces at the prime age of fifteen.

The year was 1956 and I was off to the Indian Navy, which needed young men, at fifteen years of age to sign up for a mandatory ten years. Intensive training would be offered in a technical trade and I was offered a trade in the electrical field of radio and radar. I saw my mother frail and aging after the years of struggle in life for my sake, my future, my very living, and this made me move toward this career. It would give me free clothing as uniforms, free food on a warship, training at the highest level with discipline for my good in life, and a small salary to send to my mother, who had done so much and did not desire anything in return. While on military leave, I would come to Madras, my hometown, and spend all my time with my mother, giving her the leave pay that I had saved for her. It was a small token in return for those investments that made me a grownup man after all! In faith, I was the Christian by name and family identity. Nothing more crossed my mind, as what does faith mean to a life? The hope of things to come never caused me to contemplate; the time was now—that moment only! That is what mattered.

Out of the Indian Navy after the mandatory term of ten years, it was the year 1966. This was a wonderful era in music, including the British invasion with the Beatles and the Monkees with the most popular single at the time, "I'm a Believer." It helped me to face the time ahead and helped me believe that my mother's heart was faithful always to her only child, her son, and that "GOD WILL PROVIDE." With a trade in hand from the Indian armed forces, I had great hopes for a civilian job right into the age of electronics in radio, the new generation of transistors now long forgotten. Sadly, my hopes were dashed as commercial companies in radio and electronics did not consider the armed forces training and my accredited trade to be useful in civilian business unless I had a commercial trade diploma from a commercial school for electronics. This was a divide that I could not fathom. A young man about twenty-five years in age, I was stunned by the years that had passed. My hometown, the city Madras with its slight progress, was modern, with the marvel of the jukebox, rock and roll music blaring loudly in public places, and Elvis Presley on the RCA label, the craze of record collectors and sold on black market. I had a sweet reunion with mother once again, this time staying with her. Where do you go from here? What must I do next? Will *Life's New*

Dawn be different this time, bringing about all of many unfinished longings, from my heart, to come to reality? I started searching for a job locally in the city; I thought it the best way to go! The references of my naval career, given the ten years I spent there, all had no effect. Not even a ripple in the cold hearts of employers in the commercial world, till one shop that sold Phillips, Siemens, and Grunding radios offered me a start as a field salesman, traveling within the city to sell these brand names out of his showroom. I was a youthful spirit, determined to start life anew, and each day was a challenge. Out of the throngs of people moving within the city, nearly all of us depended on our buses and commuter rail services to take us to and from places. Many of us who on many days due to poverty lacked that bus fare had one option: to walk for miles in blazing heat! The miles of black-tar roads were like a bed of live coals beneath our feet, and I covered many miles each day carrying a heavy bag with those precious radios to sell. What a pity—never did I know of an MP3 player, or a Sony Walkman radio, which would have energized me with music while walking my ways, keeping me company and high spirited. Due to limited sales and more backdoor methods of selling radios to small dealerships, the future looked bleak, stifling any possible changes to my career, as jobs were scarce. It was worth it to travel back in time and realize that my mother invested in me the rich heritage of faith as she spoke of faith in Christ as being far richer than the worldly possessions.

Faith truly stands the test of time, then and right now, years later when I am much older in age, and truly surrounded by a new day as *Life's New Dawn*. Here I am surrounded by God's goodness in the land called America. By my mother's upbringing in the very strict awareness of God, His son Christ, the cross, the resurrection, salvation, redemption in Christ, heaven and eternity, Satan, and hell for eternity were so ingrained and etched deeply into my mind. These truths made me satisfied with that knowledge. Now, years later at the age of thirty-three, I am glad that I have Christ in my heart as my personal savior. I boldly profess Him and speak of Christ to others, pointing out His love that is unlike the love from humanity, which ultimately fails at one point or another. A mother's love never fails to her children. So it was with my mother's prayers for me to tide me over through tempestuous times. God's love was steering me into the unknown of my frail thinking. God's plans are far greater than those of humans, for in Christ, as the scripture says, "For I know the thoughts that I think toward you, says the Lord. Thoughts of peace and not of evil, to give you a future and a hope" (Jeremiah 29:11). Yes, this promise was not one in vain. Changes came about from selling radios/electrical goods; changes to something greater because God was involved. What a difference from wondering each day, as I woke up, about the dread of the day I was to walk into it, with no grand sunrises to take life's breath away in awe or the hues of golden ribbons woven around the vastness of cloudless skies, as a calm, peaceful sunset, leaving me to sigh with relief that the day is done and the night has set in. What could change was that seed of doubting that always is cast in a mind no matter how strong the faith one is holding to! Scripture jumps right out in ridicule of humanity's disrespectful way of thinking. One miracle to another, the first of many was to happen. "But now thus says the Lord who created you, OH Jacob, and He who formed you, OH Israel, Fear not, for I have redeemed you, I have called you by your name. You are mine" (Isaiah 43:1). Yes, God knows my name; yes, He has called me to recognize Him more intimately, which I did not do except to know richly about God in head-knowledge only. He called to say often, "Turn your eyes upon Jesus, look full in His face, and the things of this world will look strangely dim," and more in that beautiful hymn. As time goes by, pages will unfurl, and you and I will understand how great God's hand is in our lives.I can today surely reaffirm: "MIRACLES DO HAPPEN," contrary to many who think otherwise. How about your life? Are there any miracles to wonder about that no human being in this world could have made it happen? Is it not the miracle each day that the sun rises to light up our world precisely without fail, and late in the evening the sun sets to bring that radiant glow of the moon, filling our hearts to rest and await *Life's New Dawn* in God's own special way, the next day?

LIFE'S PARTNER—
MY WIFE

A LOVE FOR A LIFETIME, a once-in-a-lifetime find, a true partner for all the days of my life on earth—I call her beloved and her name is Menuka. I call her affectionately "Minnie"! I must retrace that first moment my eyes caught a glimpse of her beauty. Yes, her beauty was breathtaking; she was a vibrant young woman with jet-black hair flowing down to her knees. Her slender, slightly tanned frame was wrapped in soft silk with brocades woven with genuine gold threads—what is known as a sari. Her delicate slender arms were adorned with gold bangles that reflected the golden glow of her face with high cheek bones, punctuated with large, almond-shaped eyes. She had a slender, graceful neck with chains decked in spirals of gold dotted with precious gems such as rubies, emeralds, and diamonds; and her earlobes reflected hues of blue and white from her diamond earrings. Ah! a perfect woman to fall in love with. My inner voice said, "Dream on! This one is far out of your reach. This is a woman who is a true work of art, as God intended when He created us." "For we are his workmanship, created in Christ Jesus, for good works, which God prepared beforehand, that we should walk in them" (Ephesians 2:10). There is the beauty in every person, as God made them.

This woman of beauty stood in the middle of a jewelry store, where she came to work to pass her time, not for her livelihood, for she manifested outwardly symbols of riches, pride, and the ladylike grace relative to her background of family, culture, the heritage, with education to top it all! She was raised to look down on the less fortunate around her. Oh! they are plentiful in India, in this city Madras, now called Chennai. My mind raced in various directions, projecting mental images of my arms holding her, to love and behold her all through my life, while it was also on fast-forward, lest I remain on pause with the beautiful picture alive before me. The picture now is of my own basic survival, with food on the table and a place to rest my weary head to dream on! How much will my dreams come true? How much will my yearnings be fulfilled?

Who can find a virtuous wife? For her worth is far above rubies. The heart of her husband safely trusts her, so he will have no lack of gain. She does him good, and not evil, all the days of her life. (Proverbs 31:10-12)

A perfect recipe for a perfect marriage. Where can I place such a tall order for such a bride, to be my life partner?

Thoughts of deep spiritual reckoning crisscrossed my mind while I was still staring at this beautiful visitor before my eyes. These are from God's word:

You made all the delicate, inner parts of my body and knit them together, in my mother's womb. Thank you for making me so wonderfully complex. It is amazing to think about. Your workmanship is marvelous, and how well I know it. You were there while I was being formed in utter seclusion. You saw me before I was born, and scheduled each day of my life before I began to breathe. Every day was recorded in your book. How precious it is Lord, to realize that you are thinking about me constantly. I can't even count how many times a day your thoughts turn toward me. And when I awaken in the morning, you are still thinking of me. (Psalms 139:13-18)

Rev. Paul Kumar

In my sight, surely out of reach, this beautiful damsel now seems so contradictory, for she is my precious wife.

This blazing star of beauty came from life's fortunate families and lived a life with no need to look outside herself for any help at all! She had deep-rooted faith in Hinduism with its gods that are graven images carved by human thinking. "The craftsman stretches out his rule, he marks one out with chalk, he fashions it with a plane, he marks it out with the compass, and makes it like the figure of a man, according to the beauty of the man, that it may remain in the house" (Isaiah 44:13). Our eyes are the honest windows to our inward souls. This young woman had the need to come out of her rich cocoon, in which she had been given instruction in the do's and don'ts even into her adult life. Her working at this electronics store was allowed to be just a pastime to break away from a deep tradition that a Hindu woman cannot step out into the world to work no matter how well educated. She should await her day in her home to be given away as a wife in an arranged marriage, the idea being that she cannot fall in love with her heart. In this case my blazing star of beauty was to be married at the end of 1968 in a Hindu marriage alliance. She had suitors and was looking for prospective men with sound education, wealth, possession of land, property, and that matched her horoscope and astrological sign, bringing all of those prerequisites in perfect alignment. By all human standards, in conclusion, would I, a Christian man, stand a chance? I had nothing to offer or brag about, except a sound head, knowledge of the Bible and scripture verses, a good moral life, and I was truly faithful to any job that enabled survival and I still could submit to the lady for the favor of her hand in marriage. "And now abide faith, hope, love, these three but the greatest of these is love" (1 Corinthians 13:13). Love: a heart of love is all that I had to offer. My heart was beating fast, racing three times faster with the need to open my soul and say, "I care about you, for your sad eyes portray the depths of your heart." Sadness amid the grand shroud of luxury in Minnie's life was solely due to the lack of family love to encircle her, rather than to the lifestyle similar to that of a caged bird desperate to find release. This beautiful songbird lost it's song of love, and needed a touch in reaching out. To reach out in my own special way, I wrote a nine-page letter weaving a love poem, words describing her entry into the store, and the poise and grace that followed as she began to work, just for fun!

With such an honest approach, by words in that letter that came to life, Minnie responded after reading that letter that she would approve of me joining her for a cup of coffee in the adjoining cafe. She spoke of her longing, after reading classic books by writers such as Thomas Hardy, Barbara Cartland, and Jane Austin, writers who were expressive in stories of romance. She always thought her life was filled with love, which, by the way, she lacked most. She wanted to be swept away by love, by a man like Prince Charming, on a white steed. As I listened to her young heart's burden, I wondered if I would be foolish enough to think that I would be that prince she was talking about, totally in contrast to many of her expectations and descriptions! It would be a farfetched accomplishment, for my situation then involved much poverty, and I dressed weirdly, as the trend of men at the time was tight pants and an Elvis hairstyle—the least that would impress her. As Prince Charming to her, imagine me just five feet four inches in height with brown skin tones, Elvis sideburns combed upward, with no chiseled facial tones either. Just plain ordinary. I could not even be added to her high school year book pictures as a friend. Within me I concluded right then and there in that coffeehouse that this true beauty was out of my reach, but I still pretended to be concerned with her conversation and her heart beating for true love—a man who would fit her expectations and offer her genuine caring and devotion, and lift her wounded spirits with healing in his actions, placing her equally in his eyes as a life partner for time immeasurable. Menuka, affectionately called Minnie, understood my Christian background with my name Paul, but my financial background hardly could compare to hers! Still, the nine-page letter from me that she read was a beautiful symphony of words, to her, come to life by my very own perceptions and impressions as she stood blazing in her beauty in the middle of that electronics store ready to work!

The brief coffee shop date was more devastating for me as the waiter presented us the bill and I looked at her with total dismay, for I could not pay for that coffee. She read through my eyes, and smilingly took her money and paid for our very first date. Wow, what a way to romance and expect things to work out my way! Devastated, I returned to work. Minnie, on the other hand, kept my nine-page letter close to her heart, cherished every word, and carried it home to her mother. Her mother was the sweet one, the confidant, as any mother is to a daughter; her deep love was as precious as any mother's on earth. She was unable to read or write English, so my letter had to be translated word for word in the local language that the family communicated with. Minnie's mother, by that very God-given instinct, could perceive where this was leading, and asked her beautiful daughter for the reason for this discussion. Was marriage in the plan for this young man, the Christian, the one who did not even come close to the many attributes within their family? Logically, practically, with true love, concern, and tears in her eyes, this mother said to Minnie, "It will not happen You are in a dream. Stop dreaming, for the consequences will be harsh and divide this family if you decide to go forth and marry this man. None of your brothers, or your admired twin sister, will ever give their approval for such a devious action!" Such powerful words from a true heartbroken mother, who on her own would have loved to have helped her daughter, so sweet and lovely, when the cruel arms of deep-seated culture—Hindu customs, traditions, wealth, pride, and arrogance— rise up to wipe away sound education, reasoning by logical minds, compassion, and well wishes for their loved one. The entire issue was now in the hands of her family elders, who would muster in the living room and query her with powerful questions, including wealth, religion, customs, habits, and living conditions after marriage, and in those categories I would fail, unable to meet their own self-proclaimed conditions, allowing Minnie go out with their approval. All this was just to impress upon Minnie that they were doing the right thing, the best for her future life. Minnie sensed conclusively that it would be a firm denial, and that serious thinking was necessary to help her family accept her final decision.

In the backdrop of a family with Hinduism as their faith, the most accepted, honorable practice was to give the hand of their daughter in marriage to a man chosen by the parents and the elders in the family. In all of the preordained customs and practices, the girl does not have a chance to dream of her man, and has no voice in the approval of her future husband and the stability of her future family and home. To dream of the man Minnie would marry was not a part of her upbringing, so all of her emotions, once locked up and almost as dry and parched as the sands of the desert, now were inspired by the thought of an oasis, a small, clear-running stream in the desert. Running toward this oasis, captured and inspired by that nine-page letter, Minnie was running toward it to be saved and to have her life—to be with a man for whom her heart beats now. His looks, his smiles, his characteristics, his antics, his humor, and a lifetime to spend with him. God in heaven still watches over His people, even those who do not know Him and acknowledge Him! I firmly believe to this day that God's extraordinary love, His unconditional love, helped this woman, who was smitten with love that no one else expressed to her! The scriptures say:

A good name is to be chosen, rather than great riches, loving favor rather than silver and gold, the rich and the poor have this in common, the Lord is the maker of them all, by humility and the fear of the Lord, are riches and honor and Life. (Proverbs 22:1-2, 4)

The hurt in Minnie was centered around her mother and her twin sister, for the bonding they grew up with. The Bible speaks of a protective mother: "She opens her mouth with wisdom and on her tongue is the law of kindness, she watches over the ways of her household, her children rise up and call her blessed" (Proverbs 31:26-28). This caring mother had her eyes filled with tears and was helpless, unable to intercede on behalf of the rest of the family. The rest of the family had already made their decision, that Minnie should be disowned by them for the reasons for her firm standing that she desired to marry Paul (me), in spite of the ensuing harsh consequences that would tear apart a family of Mom, Dad, three brothers, and the twin sister. Their feelings, kinship, and blood relationship, were shelved, allowing anger, rigid traditions, customs, and age-old beliefs to consume their hearts with hate, and she could not justify better their reasoning. Valuable education in each of them, blended with modern India social behavior, all drifted away as mist floats and becomes vapor, with the heat of their anger. To me it never made sense, even to this day, their crude, harsh, and unrealistic decision, that Minnie, a loving sister, be totally rejected, as though she never belonged to the family, and that all memories of her should be wiped away as if she were dead. Never mind God's unfurled arms were ready to grab her in and through me while I stood on the sidelines and was hurt yet determined to make it happen that Minnie would be my wife. Minnie would be my love for a lifetime, and both of us have kept that sacred, sweet promise, not for lust or worldly reasons, but in true sacredness and as a cherished promise before God and His witnesses. Our children know now that Minnie and I are two hearts woven as one, meshed in life as one, in every facet of our thinking and living, remaining for our children and grandchildren! God's supreme love was the effective bond that enabled us then to overcome hate and bitterness, with that continuing now helping us not to bear any grudges after three decades and more into our marriage and life together!

"Love will be our home." "As for me and my house we will serve the Lord" (Joshua 24:15). Minnie made the greatest sacrifice of her relationship and kinship with her precious family, the very never-to-be-broken love of a twin sister and her three brothers, all broken to pieces like the many pieces of the most valuable pottery adorning a home. What culture or tradition can turn hearts so weak? Well, the love that drew us together so strongly in the first place never weakened amid all odds; we were still bound in total admiration, never for a moment looking ahead to future consequences or circumstances but savoring the moment at hand. Isn't that the way love ought to be, when skies seem eternally blue, dispelling puffy white clouds that might sail along threatening the hush that surrounds? We both now were free to set a date when we would be by law husband and wife. Under the circumstances, with our diverse faiths, I the Christian, and Minnie the Hindu, had to reach common ground, which led us to the justice of peace at the local courthouse to file our request for a date: August 9, 1968.

What a momentous day! My joys, my emotions, my victory against the hate of this world that existed all around us. When August 9, 1968, dawned, my most beautiful lady in all of this world was at my side as the justice of peace pronounced us "man and wife"! Yes, we were two hearts so alone except for each other's arms with no family to witness the glow in our eyes, that Minnie and I belonged to each other forever, till death do us part! No fanfare with much decorations, no limousine to take us away to sandy white beaches far away, not even a cake with a topper to stand and pose in front of. No need for the world's views of how this unity in marriage was; we truly were able to hold each other without any boundaries, with tears flowing down in disbelief that we finally belonged. We looked up to heaven, asking for God's anointing, as I entrusted our lives to Him, asking of His watch and guidance for the future!

I was reminded that even at this great moment in my life—winning over the most beautiful girl in town to be my very own—I still walked about with that Christian label, with no relationship to Jesus Christ, God's son, who gave his life on a cross for my redemption to enable me to have an eternal hope for heaven when that moment of physical death comes knocking, which is sure. On the other hand, my wife, from that moment on, was still the most beautiful woman, my love who gave up so much for me. To love her included her faith in the idols of Hinduism. The Bible speaks of idols:

The metal smith stands at his forge to make an axe pounding on it with all his might. Then the woodcarver takes the axe, and uses it to make an idol. He measures and marks out a block of wood, and carves the figure of a man. Now he has a wonderful idol, that can't so much as move from where it is placed. He makes his god a carved idol. He falls down before it and worships it and prays to it. "Deliver me," he says, "You are my God." (Isaiah 44:12-17)

Such ignorance God has shut their eyes, so that they cannot see, and closed their minds from understanding. (Isaiah 44:18).

We seemed so lonely as two people ready to face the world with love to hold on, yet with poverty and uncertainty, there were lingering shadows that probably could have dimmed our hopeful hearts with fear of the unknown. I only knew best to run to the trusted aspect of prayer, for mother taught me well. Will God answer my prayer?

There is assurance, for God speaks:

Listen to me, all Israel, who are left, I have created you and cared for you since you were born. I will be your God through all your lifetime, yes even when your hair is white with age. I made you, and I will care for you. I made you, and I will care for you. I will carry you along, and be your Savior. (Isaiah 46:3-4)

God does not cast away anyone. God truly, as creator with his love, is a caring Savior for a lifetime. Minnie and I invested in our lives with each other, for we were hopelessly, helplessly alone to face the world. "Be bold, be strong; the Lord God is with you" is a part of the words to a powerful song by Morris Chapman entitled "Strong Tower." Yes, there is strength in faith, strength in cast-down hearts to rise up, and Minnie and I decided to do that. "We are pressed on every side by troubles, but not crushed and broken. We are perplexed because we don't know why things happen as they do but we don't give up and quit. We are hunted down, but God never abandons us. We get knocked down, but we get up again and keep going" (2 Corinthians 4:8-9).

Our Love is … a story from this moment on;
A chance meeting, a beauty, with a poor soul.
A short time in dating, and meeting secretly,
Learning little about each other, still sure.
Understanding at best two diverse worlds of each.
One of faith, customs, and traditions; one very simple.
It's still the story of promises to each other,
Excitement and dreams, and longings of the heart.
It's a story with no end, for it keeps on going …

Growing deeper in time, for Love becomes more certain, Beautiful with time ... One Big Romance ... for Minnie (Menuka) and Paul.

LIFE'S FIRST STEP

MAN AND WIFE, TWO AS ONE, Minnie and I, from a courthouse to a home meant for two, and we started depending on each other from then on. As it was that very first day, August 9, 1968, till this very date, thirty-seven wonderful years have passed in togetherness and sweet harmony. For my beloved wife, the first step of setting up a home was not exactly the continuation of the lifestyle of her maiden years. From whitewashed bungalows; butlers and maidservants; rich jewelry to adorn her such as gold, precious stones, rubies, diamonds; and a large circle of family—all were to be missed now! She would later realize this in looking back as if in wishful thinking or an old dream. At this very moment, she stood deserted, renounced, rejected, robbed of her family's claim of kinship for marrying me, a Christian, to them a bad "heathen"! Because of this my lovely bride's first bold step into this wedlock became slippery, uncertain, and confusing as she entered into a noisy tenement building with screams of babies and children, all in crowded rooms in partitions. There were common amenities such as one bathroom one had to stand in line taking turns to use, and one faucet for running tap water in the midst of a yard. One had to fill an earthen vessel, and this was the only water that could be used for drinking and cooking and washing clothes. Our little partition was a nook in the corner, with wafer-thin walls to give us privacy, if any; yet it was our domain for two lives that were starting so alone, left alone! That was the kind of a welcome mat for us, the two honeymooners in normal settings, on the first day after our wedding. It was unwanted, a harsh reality when you fall in love and marry, especially with deep-seated traditions and very diverse cultural bindings in faith and family such as in our case.

Our first day looking into our room was so dark, with one lonely electrical bulb hanging down from the rafters, a bare cold floor, and just outside the room was a clay oven to be used for cooking with sticks of firewood bought for a price. Speaking of price, what costs there were already just to reach this first step. My family, our loved ones, we both felt for certain would love and stand by us for the test of time; regretfully they failed, due to the deep-seated cultural position of my wife, Minnie, a Hindu.

This first step of her young life held perhaps a bright future. If it had not been for her strong-willed heart that never ceased loving the man she held high in her life—me—and her falling in love and pursuing love as her goal in her life, both of us would have fallen prey to the world's betrayal!

Sacrifices made for love surely remind me of the greatest sacrifice ever made for mankind by God: sending his own son Jesus Christ! God's love is unchanging, unconditional. He wants people to understand and believe.

Such belief gives us the confidence and hope for the day now, for tomorrow, and for the future. God's love was never reserved for one group of people because of their heritage, other faiths' social standing, or personal affluence in a community. God's love is for all who will believe in scripture. "For God so loved the world, that he gave his only begotten son, so that anyone who believes in him should not perish, but have eternal life!" (John 3:16). God's love enables us with life to live, individually believing and trusting that in mortal death, which is for sure, heaven will be our eternal home! Such a rich hope overshadows

Rev. Paul Kumar

all earthly riches, vanity, pride, and self-sufficiency, as they all will pass away at life's fleeting last breath called "death."

There is an exceeding joy and awareness, knowing, experiencing as real, that Minnie and I were as man and wife by the laws of this land—two lives woven in body, mind, and spirit as one, before God's sight to uphold the sacredness and beauty of marriage. Life's first step in each of us bears ugly scars. Poverty in my background, Minnie's helplessness and rejection by her very own family for falling in love with a Christian. We stood in somber memories of family rejection, clutching each other, not knowing what and when our next meal would be. We had no comfortable mattress with pillows to sleep on as we stood at the doorstep of this multi-tenement house, and only one small corner was ours! The cold floor with emptiness stared at our bewildered, confused faces. With my outward cloak of a Christian background, the strict upbringing of my mother, with scripture, prayers, and Bible study, brought me quality reminders from her.

She would say, "My son, never forget the things I have taught you. Never forget to be honest, truthful, and kind to others. Hold these virtues tightly close to your heart, for if you seek favor with both God and man, and a reputation for good judgment and common sense, then trust the Lord completely. Don't ever trust yourself. In everything you do put God first, and he will direct you and crown your efforts with success" (Proverbs 3:1, 3, 4-6).

I had to reassure my lady love, who sat before mute idols all her young twenty-three years of her life and whose idols were lifeless and stared back at her in a blank lifeless condition, that there is a greater person: God in the heavens, who created heaven and earth and everything else therein. From that day forward, there was the burning desire within my heart to help open those beautiful, most loving, expressive, almond-shaped eyes of hers, along with her chiseled beauty, that she might reason and enrich her wisdom and knowledge that obedience to idolatry was not helpful, and that she would understand my desire that as husband and wife we should not practice two different faiths under one roof as one household! God's word speaks to any heart that is willing to ponder and listen, and it is the first step:

For it is by believing in his heart (any heart) that a man (any person) becomes right with God, and with his (or her) mouth he (or she) tells others of his (or her) faith, thereby confirming his (or her) faith. For the scripture tells us that no one who believes in Christ will ever be disappointed! (Romans 10:10-11)

My wife's love with such trust brought her thus far, for she truly believed in falling in love with me, and was ready and willing to face life's hard knocks unlike anybody else, and to trust God in the person of Jesus Christ and not be disappointed. I by no means was above her in superior levels in my Christian walk and faith, for thought I had and walked with the head knowledge, I was spiritually lifeless, with no personal acceptance nor did I walk in life with Jesus Christ as my Savior! Minnie understood the great love of her husband and was willing to study the scriptures and the truths of the Bible.

Our days of hardships were clouded with poverty: one meal a day between husband and wife, just a bowl of rice with no side dish to flavor it, and no comforts of a real home, particularly her luxury home. Hot, humid August days with temperatures ranging from 100 to 104 degrees on the thermometer, as always, were the norm in most Indian cities. God truly loved us both, even if one did not know him, acknowledge or accept him into her life. God loved Minnie too, for he cared enough to calm our doubts, our fears, giving us a spirit of calm and no signs of despair, from that first step in life—marriage—to being life's most cherished partners, and now into our thirty-seventh year as man and wife. Yes, God does not give us greater burdens that humanly we cannot bear. God also promises that he will look after our needs.

So don't worry at all about having enough food and clothing. Why be like the heathens? For they take pride in all these things, and are deeply concerned about them. But your heavenly father already knows, perfectly well, that you need them and he will give them to you, if you give him first place in your life and live as he wants you to. So don't be anxious about tomorrow; God will take care of your tomorrow too! Live one day at a time! (Matthew 6:31-34)

For God to be in first place in our one-day-old marriage seemed the farthest thing from our minds; truly both of us were anxious about what we would eat the next day and what we would wear tomorrow, for my bride left her home to come to me with just the sari she wore around her frame of beauty! All her lavish saris and clothing were seized by her family as a part of their anger and rejection of her totally for deciding to marry a Christian, a heathen in their sight. No Samsonite suitcase or any elaborate toiletries except the sandals on her feet so as not to step on the burning asphalt roads. She was just as she was: so very beautiful, and her beauty could not be robbed of her, though she was empty handed, willing to step into uncharted waters called love and marriage. There is a beautiful Christian hymn entitled "Love Covers It All." Our love humanly as two wandering souls caught God's precious attention as he began to cover us with his coat of such loving warmth. There is scripture that says, "Stay away from the love of money, be satisfied with what you have, for God said, 'I will never, never fail you, nor forsake you'" (Hebrews 13:5-6). This is the reason why we say without any doubt or fear, "The Lord is my helper and I am not afraid of anything that mere man can do to me." With God's help, that very Christian upbringing made me respect the Bible scriptures with reverence! At this point in my life, I had not had a personal relationship with Jesus Christ as my personal Savior; I was just moving along each day and thought that heaven was a place already reserved for me because I was raised at home as a Christian by a faith-loving mother, and that it was my birthright. Such reasoning was mystified and erroneous, till the age of thirty-three when life changed me to be God's very own child. It was not too late. On the other hand, my loving wife, my partner in life, was more confused when she saw a Bible opened and read each morning, placed in our one-room abode on a wooden crate that decorated the surroundings as a center table.

There were no more clay images or idols of Hindu gods, no vain chanting of prayers, no more placing flowers to adorn the idols in the belief that these manmade, mute clay images heard the prayers. This amounted to excessive pain in her heart, and needless tears with her heavy breathing in anguish over whether she had made the right choice, falling in love with me, the Christian, and forsaking—and further by marrying me—giving up everything, including her own family. In our one-room, bare-floor apartment, we dreamed of a view, as surely it had the view of two bathrooms facing our door, for use by sixty tenement adults and children, standing in a long line to use the restroom. Our first meal was to be called lavish in that state of hardship, with a bowl of boiled rice in an earthen pot still rich with its nutrients, for the water was not drained. That rice water was supposed to be our daily ration of vitamins. No meat, no vegetables, just a raw, green chili pepper to bite and pretend that flavor was present in an otherwise very bland meal. In life we develop a lot of yearnings. In a land such as ours, America, our yearnings become more demanding for the best; for higher standards in taste and ingredients; to be bathed in much luxury, from dining to clothing to accommodations. On the other side of the world, oceans away, at a moment of what ought to be wedding bliss, we were surrounded by extreme poverty, yet longings from deep within our hearts could not be avoided. So we decided to window-shop, when our eyes caught a shop window with a display of Hunts ketchup bottles and cans of Milkmaid condensed milk, but we were unable to enjoy their contents to satisfy our longings. With no money on us, we, as husband and wife, made a must-have plan for the long-range affordability, on pay day, from my small earnings of about thirty dollars per month. With such resolve, we were able to walk away delightfully, in the joy of window-shopping! Days, weeks later we returned to that store window, hoping to buy our much-awaited bottle of ketchup and the can of sweetened condensed milk. The ketchup bottle was priced at five dollars and the can of condensed milk was priced at three dollars. In our blessed land, America, compared to India prices, Hunts ketchup is priced normally about $1.50 and a can of condensed milk about $1.25. In the words of one of our founding fathers, President Thomas Jefferson, "My God, how little do my countrymen know of what precious blessings they are in possession of, which no other people on earth enjoy." What a realization of this profound truth for two souls, my wife and I, years later in 1975, to hold on to, with all of the harsh, unexpected blows in life we were confronted with, as when her family rejected one of their own, casting away her very birthright, for no other reason than that she fell in love and married a Christian, in their reasoning a heathen! This very crude justification made my wife and I, along with our three children, faithfully uphold the truth: "For I am not ashamed of the Good News about Christ. It is God's powerful method of bringing all who believe it to heaven. This message was first preached to the Jews alone, but now everyone is invited to come to God (because of Christ, God's son) in this same way" (Romans 1:16). There is no other reason, or partiality from God, for humanity, His creation, as to nationality or background, faith, skin color, gender, looks, educational background, or social and living standard, but that genuine love is shown for all people, and that they should acknowledge God, placing their faith and trust in Him. As the scriptures say, "The man who finds life will find it, through trusting God" (Romans 1:17b).

With the dark horror of her faith in idols and her beliefs, the years of inborn habits developed within as pride, anger, looking down on others—now that she loved a man, her husband, so different in his faith, confusion gripped her mind, and she wondered, what could be done to please my husband? She often wondered if returning to her family in the same city would release her from all of the legalities and give her back her share of wealth, property, and jewelry; the luxurious settings of her home with maids, butlers, drivers, and four meals a day; the glimmer of precious diamonds and gems; saris and brocades woven with gold threads; and the greatest welcome-home party from her parents, brothers, and most of all the closest in bond, the twin sister. Surely a choice was to be made, for how long could one bear such pain from the inside to the outside, and to what extent could the actions of the heart be called "true love and devotion"?

Would all of the continued sadness, misery, and poverty end if my wife thought it best to make the choice in acknowledging Christ, to bring about the bond of a common faith in the house? Would it be better to stick it out with her honesty, sincerity, the unfathomable love for her husband, from deep within her heart. Could I forget the horror and vanity of her past world, with the darkness and ugly reminders of unforgiveness and her irreconcilable family ties, to the extent that all of her family members told others that their daughter and sister Menuka had died in an automobile crash? Minnie really wanted to experience true faith and easily made a choice herself to visit Catholic churches in the area close to our one-room abode. She had to walk miles, for all that we had was public transportation, and she did not have the bus fare! It was very commendable on her part to do what it takes to help our lives blend in common toward faith, the devotion in inseparable love for each other, and most of all, help make it work! Her immediate reaction to trying Catholicism was that she could relate to the statues of Mary, and Jesus on a cross—the very statue of Christ in a glass case with the crown of thorns, depicting the death on the cross! It surely was not the right path to her personal faith, for Christ was to be honored not Mary, and her faith to hold on was by believing and not by seeing; no form or shape, but believing from the heart, the very substance from the heart. This was no doubt the first step for her spiritual life at this point after deep practice in worshipping idols along with Hinduism and its religious demands. After Christ's resurrection, when he appeared to his disciples in the upper room, Thomas, one of the disciples, did not believe that Jesus Christ was alive and risen from the dead. The rest of the disciples confirmed seeing Jesus, saying, "We have seen the Lord!" Thomas replied, "I won't believe unless I see the nail-pierced hand, its wounds in his hands, put my fingers in them, and place my hand into his side, where Jesus was pierced with a spear, by a Roman soldier" (John 20:24-25). Minnie wanted to believe, yet desired to see before her eyes. She wanted to believe that Christ died on the cross for her sins, the stains in her life from disobedience to God, and to believe that Christ rose again from the grave to enable her to have the gift of eternal life in heaven! Minnie, in her first infant steps to understand Christianity, had a troubled spirit about inviting Christ

Rev. Paul Kumar

into her heart and her life, which was already so much like the roaring waves of uncertainty, doubt, and sadness, crashing against the rocks that gave way with no solace. Tears were flowing for her family, which was lost, and the gain of human love and promises for a bright future, yet she was filled with despair, poverty, and hardships at every turn. It was that quiet, peace, and solace that often rests within the walls of a church as people come and pray in hushed tones that she liked, and the peace within is the stillness that surrounds when in the front, near the altar of a Catholic church, lit candles create a golden glow, as each Catholic believes it is symbolic of their heart's petition, asking God to grant them by His mercy. The faithful with their heads bent low, at times lift their eyes up to look at that altar, with Jesus crucified on the cross and the statue of Mary at the side, and then out a door there is a much quieter place called the grotto, where once again the statue of Mary is in view, close enough that one can touch her silent image, kneel before her, and raise a prayer that they believe she can intercede on one's behalf. How strange, Christ is our intercessor who pleads on our behalf to the Father in heaven. Minnie's curious eyes and searching heart absorbed all of this as she moved within the Catholic church with respect and reverence. She needed the exposition of the truth in the Gospels, God the Father, God the Son, God in His Holy Spirit, and all three in one as the blessed Trinity. Minnie felt consoled in her own special ways for seeking spiritual belonging as she cried tears from deep within her heart to the statue of Mary, the earthly mother of Jesus of Nazareth, and she felt that her cries would be noted with compassion, that of a woman like Jesus's mother (every mother is blessed with compassion) and that all answers would come. Actually Minnie needed to hear that God's grace will come from heaven, as she believed that God surely loved her, and Christ, God's son, first loved her and died on the cross at Calvary for her, that she might believe in Jesus Christ, the way, the truth, and the life, and that there is no other way or means of understanding the profound truth! I, as a Protestant Christian, did not by any means share such powerful yet simple truths to help her divide the real and easy steps to know Jesus Christ as her Savior. I was equally lacking that awareness within me, for I was covered with that cloak of what was taught to me by my faithful mother, who did not go a step further to explain that Christ desires a personal relationship with him and not just the head knowledge. Minnie needed to believe by her faith, not by sight, in Christ! Jesus came to the upper room a second time, and this time Thomas the disciple was present. Jesus said, "Thomas, put your finger into my hands. Put your finger into my side. Don't be faithless any longer. Believe!" Then Jesus told him, "You believe because you have seen me, but blessed are those who haven't seen me, and believe anyway" (John 20:27, 29). Scripture taught me to have my faith in Jesus Christ, in His death on a cross for my sins, in His victory over death, in His resurrection, and His offer of forgiveness for my sins and the sins of all who will believe. What about Minnie, my beloved wife, tossed about in her wisdom and mind? What is the truth, and how could she comprehend the word "faith"? What is faith? It is the confident assurance that something we want is going to happen. It is the certainty that what we hope is waiting for us, even though we cannot see it up ahead. By faith, by believing in God, we know that the world and the stars, in fact all things, were made by God's command, and they were all made from things that can't be seen (Hebrews 11:1, 3). Minnie needed strong assurances at this point in her life, much loving with kindness, and true compassion looking into her heart tossed with fears, desires for the truth, and strength within her to say yes to a Savior who was willing and ready to own her as His very own child! From that infantile faith in me, the Christian by name, from that year of 1968, the year of our marriage, I today am able to understand, know, and speak about the power of God, the scriptures, spiritual reasoning, and wisdom and experience God's hand in working my life and the life of our own household each day. God made good use of me, even with the outward label as a Christian. He made me an open vehicle, and helped me to be of support to my young, vibrant, educated wife, and to help her by speaking of God as best as I could and to help erase the disillusionment in her confused mind as she desired to grasp Catholicism, with its statues of Christ, Mary, and the apostles. I made her aware of how Jesus spoke of prayer: "But when you pray go away by yourself, all alone and shut the door behind you, and pray to your heavenly father secretly, and your father who knows your secrets will reward you" (Matthew 6:6). God desires that we talk to him, directly with him, as a child would talk to a father, with no one in between to mediate. As best as I was taught, and knew, of that foundation, I desired that Minnie would arrive at that point of reckoning, to believe and accept that "Jesus is the way, the truth and the Life. No one comes to the Father except through me" (John 14:6).

Minnie began picking up the copy of the Bible in our home left on a wooden crate that served as a center table, and started reading the New Testament chapters and focused on many scriptures that I had underscored with a yellow marker as highlights. It began as daily devotional, which was like nourishment to a starved soul, or dewdrops fresh and pure to a dry piece of land, choked with the dry thistles of weeds and thorny vines constantly choking the very inward desire to know more about a living God! She wanted to believe so much that "Jesus was the answer" and not the mute idols that stared back at her for twenty-three years of her young life! From that very "first step" in our lives as husband and wife in 1968, the love, devotion, respect, togetherness, and leaning on each other for comfort, solace, joy, and peace became that intimate dependency, wanting to understand life better and know its course for us ahead, and the cruel, crooked pathways that came to steer us away from honest living.

The love between us never lost it's luster; instead, it brought about a stronger assurance that everything is going to be all right in Jesus Christ as our God in our hearts and our home. Our marriage was sacred, as our hearts believed, even though the legality was with the justice of peace. Somehow God brought out in us a very good and worthy lesson to learn in caring for and sharing with others, no matter what our lives could afford. The only income for us came from my working for an electrical company, selling electrical goods to building contractors. This very lesson that I am about to share with you was so valuable as a "first step" when God brought forth a miracle in return. It was a very hot, humid summer's day, as India has only two seasons in the year: summer and winter, no spring or fall. I walked great distances to board the city's buses to travel from place to place, carrying in both my arms heavy bags with electrical items to sell as part of my job. With the roads boiling to a point of temperatures as high as 104 degrees Fahrenheit, there was this beggar man who was scantily clad, and his bare chest was exposed with twelve ribs. He had a bony frame with matted hair, as though it was glued to his head, for lack of a bath and grooming. He hastily approached me with his outstretched hands, asking for money, and in my poverty, I barely had the necessary coins for my bus fare while on the job. My immediate reaction was that deep within my heartstrings tugged pity and concern for this unknown man on the street, a panhandler, near where I lived. To help this starving man, I took a piece of paper and briefly wrote a note asking Minnie to part with my only meal, a bowl of rice with water and no other flavoring. That was the only meal for us once a day, cooked in an earthen pot. The bowl of cooked rice was very enticing as we parted. As my wife recanted this gesture, her reaction to my note was that she did not understand how I could give away my only meal to a stranger, with no further thinking that it was the only meal for us for that day. She was gracious, and acted upon my note, by asking the panhandler to sit down and have his (our) meal! Having gone through this moment, the panhandler in turn expressed his thanks, saying that husband and wife had graciously shared the meal with him and that God would bless our home! The stranger went his way, never to be seen again. Many years hence, with Jesus Christ in our hearts, Minnie and , pondered over the scripture in Matthew 25:42-45:

"For I was hungry and you gave me no food, I was thirsty, and you gave me no drink, I was a stranger and you did not take me in, naked and you did not clothe me, sick and in prison you did not visit me." Then they will also answer him saying, "Lord when did we see you hungry, or thirsty, as a stranger, or naked or sick, or in prison, and did not minister to you?" Then He will answer them saying, "Assuredly I say to you, inasmuch as you did not do it, to one of the least of these, you did not do it to me!"

To this day I have thought much of that fleeting encounter with that beggar and my innocent responses, my actions that showed kindness. I will never know who that man was! Minnie, my wife, never questioned my actions, to part with the only meal of the day; she truly agreed to the unity in our thinking, the wish and desire in her heart to help the needy, to accept the truth that God loved her as much! Jesus said, "It is more blessed to give than to receive" (Acts 20:35b). From this one-time happening, Minnie and I learned a very valuable lesson. God will provide for us. Scripture reminds us, "For this is commendable if because of conscience toward God one endures grief, suffering wrongfully. For what credit is it when you are beaten for your faults, you take it patiently? But when you do good and suffer for it, if you take it patiently, this is commendable before God" (1 Peter 2:19-20). Life's blows buffeted me, the husband, and I was unable to provide much for a love who, for my sake, suffered blows in total rejection from a large family, with a mom, dad, three brothers, and most of all, a twin sister. Wrongful suffering, perhaps, asking for nothing but acceptance of her love of someone other than of their choosing by compulsion to marry.

With the pain and anguish of how our lives began as husband and wife, both of us were feeling more like we were not alone; but God's love was in our midst, and he wooed our hearts to do what is right. We felt an anticipation strangely, that God in His own pleasure changes, reshaping our lives, with strides to go forward, and all that we were going through and sharing together was not time lost as married life.

Life's new hope, as in chapter 2, was one to remember. It brought much relief there in India, with grim reminders of life beginning. Love, blind you may say, was still the most powerful ingredient, and a bond that kept hope in our hearts afresh each new day. With the trust we had in each other, with the reverence for God and respect for people who came our way, we stood with that fervent Hope that someday with God's help, life would take a new turn full of meaning and purpose with God in control, steering our future. We desired a family to fill the void of family lost in Minnie's young life. With our own children, who are a blessing, life would give us greater joys and meaning, and afford us the heritage that Minnie and I could not claim! "It is a wonderful heritage to have an honest Father" (Proverbs 20:7). The love of a mother excels and she lavishes it upon her children. The father becomes a strong tower, for he finds shelter in the blessings of the Lord. Each moment, our inward wounded hearts were softened by God's compassion, mercy, and favor. Minnie and I were truly two lonesome souls marooned, moving with caution in a land called India, a city called Madras, now known as Chennai. We had a sad mixture of pride, prejudice, poverty, riches, deep-seated traditions, culture, customs, and habits, firmly refusing change even as time progressed into a very modern world! In life even a toddler stumbles, falls down, and crawls, until a day in the future when the toddler is able to stand up, to plant both feet firmly on the ground, and show the world "life's first steps."

LIFE'S NEW HOPE

HOPE IN LIFE IS SO NECESSARY, especially in faraway countries such as India, where poverty prevails and any average worker creates a deep chasm of struggle to just tide himself over, while the wealthy rise to a higher financial and social standing. What an imperfect setting and an imbalance in society. Here I was struggling, after my naval tenure of ten years, to get back into a civilian environment, hoping for a decent job, and I end up selling radios and electronic goods. A friend saw a classified in the local papers for airline jobs and truly suggested that I try. Air India was the national airline, and still is today. Working for them was furthest from my thoughts, yet intrigue stepped into my mind, and I wondered if it would be worth attempting to apply. I picked up an application form from their city ticket offices and attached a very brief résumé, since there was not much in my working life to speak about as experience. The moment arrived when I had to take written tests at various local hotel venues on Air India's policies, and had to pass each round leading to the next level. Then came the time for personal interviews before a panel of judges, as a part of the distilling process when thousands like me applied for a limited number of opportunities for jobs. Normally in the job market in India, when the jobs are of higher standards like this one for an airline, success can come if a person is in contact with high-ranking government officials, ones from the public sectors, or someone who is just plain wealthy or notoriously known to speak about you to the prospective employer. With no such luxury of recommendations on my behalf, nor was I outspoken in that city of thousands of people like me milling about on its streets, I literally was a "nobody"! Scripture is to many, as it is to me, the only framework to hold on to, as God portrays himself in so many facets that relate to life. Often people reject it, as I would have if I had not known better, even as head knowledge, and if my mother had not made sure I learned it from an early age. Head knowledge brings good awareness too, and it does here as God says: "The Lord said to me, 'I knew you before you were formed within your mother's womb; before you were born, I sanctified you and appointed you as my spokesman to the world'" (Jeremiah 1:5). That was one plan among the many to follow as I unraveled each precious time in my life to bring about hope to you, as "life's new hope" means truth in every sense of the word!

So with the end of "life's new hope," which began with human doubting, in me slowly it looked worthwhile to dream, and from that dream, God nudged me to move into reluctant actions allowing me to shine in His blessings. Finally I became a proud, qualified recruit as a customer service agent for the national airline of India—Air India! The year 1969 marked a new step in my life, that of my true love, my wife Minnie, and we were overwhelmed with joy, unable to contain it within our hearts. In both of us faith did not play the primary role, as it should have, witnessing events of providential nature happening right before our eyes. Spirituality took a back seat, except the methodical moving within and outside the house, calling myself a Christian and our family a Christian home. It would not have the slightest meaning, nor it's effervescent power of love, till Minnie and I along with everyone who would believe that "God so loved the world that He gave His only begotten Son, that whomever believes in Him, should not perish, but have an everlasting Life" (John 3:16). My mother's prayers were as mile markers to chart distances as I walked on life's pathways to help God

Rev. Paul Kumar

protect me, keep me strong amid life's cruel blows. With this newfound success, our financial outlook was stronger with my much higher salary, which helped us to move into our own private home, a rented house by the airport. God's smiles mark life-changing events in any life, especially for Minnie and me, as we wanted and were blessed with our firstborn child, a boy, whom we named Victor—"Victorious" maybe, for Mom and Dad stuck to the course that God silently steered them on without any fanfare from heaven. Each day at the airport departure counters, I would look upon the faces of the throngs of people leaving our shores of India, to settle down in distant lands such as the United Kingdom, Australia, Singapore, and Malaysia for a better future. It did on occasions stir envy within me, forgetting the strengths afforded my wife and I with our newborn baby right there at home! I also marveled at the advancements in technology, the marvel of those huge silver birds that flew high above. Air India's Jet age began, from the sleek Boeing 707 jets with powerful Rolls-Royce engines, to the next advancement of the Boeing 747, the jumbo jet, that joined the fleet. They towered three stories high above the ground as I stood on the tarmac, and I was always grateful and thanked God routinely, as I was taught to pray. Two years now had progressed and with this airline came a strange twist in that placid life of comfort and stability in which all was well, when Air India announced that new employees who were temporary awaiting permanent status would not be upgraded, thereby avoiding company benefit plans such as overtime, medical benefits, and wage increases due to seniority and merit performance. This seemed a blow to me, as I worked hard and was observed to be dedicated by my own airport manager. God stepped in once again, as the airport manager spoke to me about his personal concern about me and said that it was best to leave the airline at this opportune time because a good friend of his, a manager at a local travel agency of great repute, desired I go to work for him. In observing me at the airport desk, this travel agency manager truly wished that I were at his agency and not working for the airline. Such an impression of me helped me to make my decision and leave Air India to work for this well-known travel agency in town. Yes, it would be a gain, not a loss, of stability in a job, and with fairly the same amount in salary. Side by side, there came this thought of why any sane person would leave an airline job, from the top of the ladder of progress, and hurry downward to the bottom to a travel agency, from where most travel professionals begin their journey. The answer to the travel agency was yes, and I went to work for them. The year was 1970, and God's thoughts for my family and me were higher: "This plan of mine is not what you would work out, neither are my thoughts the same as yours. For just as the heavens are higher than the earth, so are my ways higher than yours, and my thoughts than yours" (Isaiah 55:8-9). The individual spiritual growth to be aware of and to act upon that Minnie, my wife, and I individually needed was the truth that we are able to ask forgiveness for all our actions of disobedience toward God: "Yes all have sinned, all fall short of God's glorious ideal, yet now God declares us 'not guilty' of offending him if we trust in Jesus Christ, who in his kindness takes away our sins" (Romans 3:23-24). We were wrapped up in our own methods of sorting out our problems, concerns, fence mending, and taking each stride as it came along in personal gratification, for we made it to such heights, in and amid the poverty-stricken world around us, that Minnie and I forgot so soon that we two were of them, among them, just down the road on memory lane! How soon vanity can take hold of even the strongest faithful heart! In all such human pride, humans set God aside. Christ never does; he is ever patient, waiting for our hearts to turn. "So look upon your old sin nature as dead, and unresponsive to sin, and instead be alive to God, alert to him, through Christ Jesus our Lord" (Romans 6:11).

As a family it is of wonderment to look upon my wife of thirty-seven years and see how she has enriched my life, standing on the promises of those vows that were spoken in 1968 when I said to her, "To cherish and to hold, for better or worse, for rich or poor, in sickness or in health, for all the days of my life!" Barriers of beliefs restrict the intentions of the heart that yearns for truth. Caste systems, cruel customs, habits, ignorance to equality, and fairness for one to decide create such diversity amid individuals and families. To the one whom I love and owe my life greatly, the sanctity and the holiness of marriage was of value, man to woman. God began to work in her heart. Here she was in 1968, a bright young woman of twenty-four years of age; a Hindu by birth, she rested her faith in idols, worshipping them daily, seated before them devotedly chanting her prayers. She had a greater circle of family, unlike me, the only child. She had her parents; three educated, well-placed businessmen as brothers; and most of all, the twin sister, who was to be a tower of strength. It makes one wonder about sitting down to worship many idols with such dedication to the faith. All her wealth, affluence, and diversity stepped in, playing a cruel hand in her life when a Christian man walked into her life, filled with love, desire, admiration, and longing to belong to each other without any second thoughts. Christian ways were a part of her school life in her days in the English schools, a place for higher learning and values, which her wealth afforded her. Education is vitally the key to greater knowledge and wisdom to anyone, as it opens and illumines minds with reasoning, turning ambitions, challenges, and dreams in good for life's issues. Contrary to such possibilities, in my wife her family's mindset influenced her until we met and fell in love, and in rebellion walked away from age-old traditions such as inhibitions. All of us are no exception; no matter what background we have in faith, until the skies open from above and let heavenly rain soak us, reminding us to look up above, all good things work for those who love the Lord. "For it is God who works in you, both to will and to do for His good pleasure" (Philippians 2:13). Because of our diverse faiths, as husband and wife with a newborn baby we needed to experience God's love, which we failed to take note of.

"God demonstrates his own love toward us, in that while we were still sinners, Christ died for us" (Romans 5:8). The was year 1969, and I now was working with the travel agency. The short-lived career at Air India was one that made me realize, much later in life, that is was the stepping-stone to the most cherished crucial step to life's onward journey. With so much left behind and with a clearer understanding of one's faith, Minnie, my beloved wife, and I separately realized we needed to come to a common ground in accepting Christ as our Savior. "Therefore if anyone is in Christ, he (or she) is a new creation, old things have passed away, behold all things have become new" (2 Corinthians 5:17). Life anew in faith, compared to life anew in our jobs, still made us put off our actions in proceeding and grasping the truth. "For it is God who commanded light to shine (at creation) out of darkness, who has shone in our hearts, to give the light of the knowledge of the glory of God in the face of Jesus Christ" (2 Corinthians 4:6). Thousands fled from India to distant lands, and little did I know that my turn was about to come to help me take hold of "life's new hope!" How would it become reality? None would understand, for the method and the means by which hope became so real much later that held all of us spellbound, still does today with wonderment and emotions that make tears of thankfulness flow down when retold over and over again by our own family to strangers. Our firstborn child, a son, Victor, was growing up well, at which time I was able to enjoy a trip on Air India, all expenses paid, for seven days to the Far East; places such as Tokyo, Osaka, Hong Kong, Kuala Lumpur, Bangkok, and back. This trip was to familiarize travel agents with such exotic destinations in the world, for which I was chosen, having been once a part of the airline itself, and also as a travel agent who would sell such destinations. The trip was more meaningful than my visits to many seaports during my naval career aboard India's warships. From sailor to travel agent now made a load of difference in comparison. With very limited funds, I surely came home after my trip with toys from abroad for my baby Victor and clothing and good things to adorn my lovely wife, also the first priority, and this made me so very glad and complete. What a big memory awakening for my mother, who always reassured me, in my early childhood and throughout my growing up, that "God will provide." Surely he did more than that; he enabled me to bask in the luxury of the things of my heart's desire, not of my heart in His control.

LIFE'S AWAKENING

THE POWER OF GOD'S WORD IS AN AWAKENING to anyone who has no place to go except to hold on to the one you love and say, "If I could be anywhere in the world, I'd rather be me, so in love at your side, always." With all of the twists and turns of our lives, those of Minnie and Paul, there was this moment in time when my faith-loving mother asked me to read a certain verse in the Bible: "For I am God, I only, and there is no other like me, who can tell you what is going to happen. All I say will come to pass, for I do whatever I wish" (Isaiah 46:9-10). It was of no impact at that time, in the year 1969 to 1970. Today upon reflection, those two scripture verses form the basis of all of what God desired to accomplish in his desire for our lives, having watched us from the start, two souls so much in love, now man and wife. God's love stands above all else, as scripture says, "Understand therefore that the Lord your God is the faithful God, who for a thousand generations keeps his promises, and constantly loves those who love him and who obey his commands" (Deuteronomy 7:9). From the star of our lives in a one-room tenement building, surrounded by the screams of babies and children and with no privacy, we went to live in our own rented home, and I had a new job at the airport in Madras. Working for Air India was a humbling experience, not one for the ego, but one of deep gratitude and dedication to my employers. From the past routines of having one meal a day, we began to have three well-organized meals, with sauces, meats, and vegetables. With a certain calm in our lives, we earnestly prayed for our child, the firstborn, to be a blessing from God in our lives. "You will be blessed above all the nations of the earth, not one of you, whether male or female shall be barren, not even your cattle" (Deuteronomy 7:14).

God answered our prayers, and in July 1970 our first child, a boy, was born, and we named him Victor. God was allowing us to make each year a momentous one. He was bringing about changes to our lives to help us understand that no other human being was involved, but him alone. At this juncture, scripture confirms: "I the Lord, the God of Israel, the one who calls you by your name, I called you by name when you didn't know me. I am Jehovah, there is no other God. I will strengthen you and send you out to victory even though you don't know me." How much more love can God show to us, with all of His creation around us, the wonders that came into being, which is truly life's awakening? Working with the airline Air India, I was dreaming of a very settled life, the joy of our firstborn son, being a husband and father, and being able to support the family. It surely was a world of difference, going from working in an electrical store to a prestigious airline career, and I was grateful to God for the imbedded spiritual upbringing of my dear mother. It was the driving force of my life. It seemed that I was breeding within me selfish desires, selfish thinking, all centered around me, my wife, my firstborn baby, and not beyond my walls of moderate, comfortable living. From the airline job, due to uncertainties I went to work for a travel agency that later would prove to be the awakening, the stepping-stone to unimaginable miracles from heaven above! Often in my human ways of disbelief, God had to nudge and remind me, as in the scriptures: "Don't forget this, guilty ones, and don't forget the many times I clearly told you what was going to happen in the future, for I am God, I only, and there is none like me, who can tell you what is going to happen. All I say will come to pass, for I do whatever I wish" (Isaiah 46:8-10). This was a powerful chastening

Rev. Paul Kumar

reminder to me as I drowned with doubts and misconceptions over my decision to change jobs to go work for a travel agency. The agency, having known about me from my performance with Air India, the national airline, placed me as a travel coordinator to exclusively be responsible for all travel arrangements for the chairman of this large textile manufacturer once owned by the British when they ruled India prior to India's independence in 1947. To add to such an esteemed assignment at this travel agency, I was also responsible for customers who sought travel within India, the domestic routes. To help visualize this agency, I must talk of how this travel unit belonged to this huge textile manufacturing company, so as to cater to in-house travel for their own officers, and with success they decided to open their doors to the public as well! With that, this agency was also the American Express-authorized mail collection center for tourists passing through Madras, India! This agency was one of those that catered to locals and foreigners in the big city.

One hazy summer afternoon, an elderly foreign tourist walked in the agency and first went to look for his mail, as he was in transit, and then pulled up a chair to sit before one of our experts who attended to international travel needs exclusively. Taking a few moments in that area, this tourist dressed in khaki shorts and a straw hat, in order to be comfortable with the sweltering heat of the city, Madras, got up and came in my direction—to my desk—to enquire about travel arrangements within India, on a domestic route. With that, this tourist also spoke of the need to have other tickets in his itinerary for travel between Madras and Sri Lanka, and then the final part of his trip to this part of the world, to return home from Bombay to New York via JFK Airport. After a brief conversation about the tourist's needs, he also remarked how my colleague at the international desk was not too happy to help him, for it was time to close; working hours for our agency ended at 5 p.m.

Sensitive to that statement, this tourist thought it best to come to my desk hoping for better service, as his first flight out of Madras was to be early the following morning. I reassured the tourist of my willingness to stay and attend to his travel needs. Patiently, as he sat before me, I worked out every detail of his itinerary, and the next part of the international tickets was on British Airways, whose offices were not open until the next morning. They also closed at 5 p.m., and here we were after 5 p.m., working on his immediate travel needs. This tourist would be gone by the time I could help complete the ticketing from British Airways the next day. We devised a plan and agreed that I would obtain that part of his ticket and take the responsibility of sending it in an envelope through India's domestic airline, Indian Airlines, care of the duty office, to the airport where he would arrive per his prepared itinerary. My honest, factual presentation developed a true sense of goodwill, trust, and his personal impressions of my sincere handling of his travel needs! When he sat before me face to face, there was no time for friendly conversations personally, just the business part. I could not tell if my customer was from the U.S. All I caught was a glimpse of him; he was a foreign tourist. Later on until today, in retrospect that day in 1970 was a red-letter day that God used in totally changing the course of my life, and it truly awakened all the dead senses within my heart to the fact that he was in control. Who was this tourist, with no radical differences from the others who came in each day, and then are gone? Once again God's word: "I will call that swift bird of prey from the east, that man Cyrus from far away. He will come and do my bidding. I have said, I would do it and I will" (Isaiah 46:11). Truly, what does this reassurance mean, and does it have any relevance to my life? The big difference is that I in my limited human thinking, much trodden down for most of my life, could not think further than my limited boundaries that held me captive to distrust, stalemate, and a lack of dreaming; I had no fresher outlook on life except to be firmly grounded to the present, not to look beyond into the future. Simply put, I was content. "A job well done!"

Two years later in 1972, still diligent and hardworking at the travel agency, I gained a lot of popularity from my peers. I was also blessed with an all-expenses-paid trip by Air India to the Far East. With the luxury of that familiarization trip for seven days, I had returned with gifts for my beloved wife and my newborn son. Saris that an Indian woman drapes around herself truly bring forth the beauty of a national costume. Toys from Japan and Hong Kong were an added luxury for my newborn son. Speaking of the sari, painful memories came rushing back of when my beloved wife was sent out of her home in 1968, rejected and renounced by her family because she was in love with me, the Christian man, and because of her decision to marry me. Everything that was taken away from her, including her personal clothing called saris! She just walked out with just the one that was draped around her, for without it she would have lost her only precious possession ... modesty ... amid a cruel world! As in the first year of our marriage, we were held down by the fierce undercurrents of harsh poverty. I could not buy new clothing such as saris for my wife. As necessity compelled her, she learned to sew, and used old jute sacks in which rice was marketed to shops that would throw them away after emptying the rice. Those jute sacks became her undergarments, sewn with a large, oversized needle, and draped on her one sari in her possession, after so many repeated washes to get it clean. Just to think of the courage in her, for the sake of love and nothing else, stirs within me anger and awareness of human injustice, and hatred for people who judge if one does not fit into their mould, cast them out! This moment was so different from my return from the trip abroad, bearing gifts that outclassed and outdid the jute sacks and the cardboard boxes that were imaginary toy trains for my baby!

With the joys of returning home to Madras, India, after a trip so fulfilling, I went back to work, when at the travel agency there was a letter waiting for me from the U.S. I was surprised to see the envelope correctly addressed to me, bearing an address in North Carolina. I opened the envelope nervously, looking at the stationery with a travel agency's name printed as Brasstown Travel service , Hayesville, North Carolina. I could not link this letter to any events of that time and wondered why it had come from the U.S. when I did not even have a pen pal there. Here again, with no hope beyond the moment at hand, saturated deep with hopelessness in the mind, I somehow managed to read the lines of that letter. The writing became alive as this person expressed his gratitude for my services rendered at the travel agency, when he had sat before me at my desk two years earlier, having all of his airline tickets taken care of. He wrote of his travel, an uninterrupted trip and of my envelope with his international tickets that were at the right airport awaiting his pickup to travel finally toward the New York (JFK) airport to head home. I could not place Hayesville, North Carolina, on a map of the U.S. but I know more now about the area of western North Carolina, across North Georgia, where near a town called Hiawassee stands this beautiful town of Hayesville. This gracious thank-you letter, two years after that red-letter day when this man came to my town Madras, India, had more to say; with detailed business proposals, he asked that I consider working for him at his travel agency in Hayesville, North Carolina. He spoke of his offer based upon the impressions left in his mind of the kind of customer care, attentiveness, and completion of the job he required, which summed up a good candidate to work for him.

The offer of employment in this letter was that this tourist agency owner would file for my Department of Labor certification and immigration status as a permanent resident, along with my family. He also spoke of the salary in U.S. dollars, and fully prepaid tickets to be ready for the flights to the U.S. when the visas were granted by the local U.S. Consulate offices in Madras. With total disbelief, tears welled up in my eyes, and I did not know how to treat this letter, a polite thank-you note, or a serious proposal to act upon from my side with a reply desired expediently. Once more God reminded me and memory rekindled the beauty of scripture (Isaiah 46:9-11). Further, another scripture came knocking into memory: "For I am offering you my deliverance, not in the distant future, but right now. I am ready to save you, and I will restore Jerusalem and Israel, who is my glory" (Isaiah 46:13). True to God's promises, he does restore broken hearts, our broken dreams, by allowing his loved ones to experience brokenness first, not knowing what the future holds! I took this opportunity to respond to this letter, which I first discounted and remarked was a

Rev. Paul Kumar

polite thank you. The scriptures in Isaiah 46:9-11, 13 haunted me about how God was indeed making a way when one thinks there is no way; God provides the means in ways one cannot understand. This kind of reasoning made me respond favorably, willing to accept the offer. This man who had met me as a visitor in Madras, India, two years earlier had his arms outstretched in welcome to me and my family to cross over the oceans to a land called America, a land blessed to be full and plentiful, founded by great men of faith who allowed God to work as a nation with prayer, deep faith, and the scripture as a foundation. Much of God's goodness is humanly forgotten in the land today. It is time to briefly speak of this man from the U.S. now as a benefactor.. He was a bachelor, well mannered, very articulate in his speaking, an astute businessman, and a community leader in the western North Carolina town of Hayesville. He was also a generous philanthropist; he supported and was surrounded by loving people in the same community of Hayesville. He was an ideal personality that the world looked up to, that defined goodness and success. One inborn quality unnoticed, or not ever talked about, was his personal faith as he moved around. He did not believe in God, His creation, or God's handiwork of nature and beauty, from the backdrop of the Blue Ridge Mountains to the lush green valleys dotted with homes in Hayesville along Highway 64, running straight and connecting towns along the way up to Asheville, North Carolina. With this dream now of great promises waiting to burst forth in reality—going to America—hopes took deeper control within our household. With my willingness to accept the offer of employment, many letters to the respective government authorities were exchanged, with procedures followed for the Department of Labor certification and requests made to the Department of Immigration and Naturalization for permanent residency in the U.S. The local U.S. Consulate in Madras, my hometown, was also well advised of the proceedings. Every step was taken, and the moment arrived for the visas to be issued, when the local U.S. Consulate's office remarked of a long delay due to so many on a list waiting for travel to the U.S. at various levels of status, including permanent residency. The consulate indicated that delays could last up to three or five years. I could only hope that our travel would be around the year 1975. When human efforts, even the honest, sincere ones, fail, there is hope in God's word. I am the Christian man, the one with all the head knowledge of the Bible, prayer, and scripture verses in memory, without a personal responsive acceptance of Christ God's son as Savior in my life. Still God in His unfailing Love pointed out, "For I know the plans I have for you, says the Lord. They are plans for good and not for evil, to give you a future and a hope. In those days when you pray I will listen. You will find me, when you seek me, if you look for me in earnest" (Jeremiah 29:11-13). Minnie and I had to cling to such a foundation as one overboard in distress would cling for life to a life raft, tossing about aimlessly, looking up above to the heavens that God would be our safety. We also watched for the rich hues of God's promise painted across a clear blue sky: the rainbow, where there will be no more dark clouds with rain coming down in the form of disappointments, and tears in response to circumstances that we could not control. Minnie and I clung to each other for emotional strengths; that the love so dear that had bound us together would also be the love to hold us now. My beloved wife, Minnie, at this point in her life was still very unsure of the direction in which her personal faith would be found. From her past in Hinduism, with idol worship for all of her young life of twenty-three years, now married to a Christian, she took the road to Catholic faith. It seemed likely, in the way her thinking was, to observe statues of Mary, Jesus's earthly mother, in an area of the Catholic church with surrounding lush greenery, quiet, and calm for a troubled mind; it seemed ideal where woman to woman she felt her tears would be understood. Minnie felt that Mary would be the heavenly power, as she saw her in the form of a statue that would intercede to Christ in heaven on our behalf. Actually Mary was the earthly mother, whom God found favor in to conceive the heavenly baby as a virgin for bringing into the world God's only Son, Jesus Christ. Scripture portrays that virgin conception as God's favor rested upon her. In scripture: "And having come in the angel said to her, 'Rejoice, highly favored one, the Lord is with you, blessed are you

Rev. Paul Kumar

among women'; Then the angel said to Mary, 'Do not be afraid, Mary, for you have found favor with God.'" (Luke 1:28 and 30). It was not clear to Minnie then that God's favor is always readily there for us to pray directly to Him, and that there is no need for any intermediary to plead our cause. The model prayer, the Lord's Prayer, underscores God to be found, His abode heaven, and His son Christ, who in heaven pleads on our behalf when we pray, "Our father in heaven, hallowed be thy name" (Matthew 6:9-13). Spiritually my beloved wife was longing on her own, with no coercion from me, her own husband, to force her to accept the Christian faith. God in his care was already preparing her heart, as wet grounds with soil ready for the seeds of faith in Jesus Christ to be planted. The year was 1975, and with human understanding and patience to its highest order. My prospective employer at one stage was losing his patience waiting endlessly for our visas. He wrote me a letter saying the offer of my employment with his agency would be withdrawn if my family and I were not in the U.S. at a certain date given by him. We were helplessly caught midstream between two governments, the long list of prospects like me, also desiring to be in the land of the free and the brave, America. I, in my human efforts or power, could not sway any one side to be successful and gain visas to travel right away. God's plan was truly different for our frustrations and our hopelessness. So came another letter from my employer, after rethinking the issues at hand, stating that the offer of employment with his travel agency would be left open for a lifetime in the hope that our visas would be granted, allowing us to travel to the U.S.

The powerful scriptures of Isaiah 46:9-11 and 13 relate to God's unique way of allowing strangers in our lives to work for His plans for our good. In the Bible, God spoke to a pagan king named Cyrus, "When I say of Cyrus, he is my shepherd, he will certainly do as I say, and Jerusalem will be rebuilt, and the temple restored for I have spoken it" (Isaiah 48:28). God will rebuild and restore individual lives, the lives of families, or as in our case, stranded, awaiting for heavenly grace to shower us. Even though Cyrus was a pagan king, he was the instrument of God's purpose in the lives of his people. There was a reason, and a mission to be completed, for God said so! Once again scripture speaks: "And why have I named you for this work? For the sake of Jacob my servant, Israel my chosen. I called you Cyrus by name when you didn't know me. I am Jehovah and there is no other God. I will strengthen you and send you out to victory even though you don't know me" (Isaiah 45:4-5). My reasons for having God's word interwoven truly makes my heart stand still, as well as to hear the actual spoken words of God at my side, telling me at each stage how things are shaping up! Do you agree? I hope so!

The day arrived when our permanent-residence visas were given so that we could make our plans to travel to the United States of America. Jubilant spirits, humbled by personal experiences and patience for three long years while seeking God's help, praying, pleading, and writing to the employer to keep hopes alive, finally had arrived! The news felt as welcome as the fresh morning dew in small droplets stinging our faces like little needles to awaken us truly to "LIFE'S AWAKENING"! I immediately wrote about our plans and requested the airfares be prepaid, which was a part of the employment offer.

During those three years of waiting—from 1972 when the letter arrived in Madras at the travel agency where I had served this man to the year 1975 when our visas were handed to us—I prematurely was too confident in leaving India for the U.S. I resigned from where I worked in Madras, and found myself in a dilemma when the U.S. Consulate advised me of a three-year wait for visa consideration to be a permanent resident in the U.S. I had lost my only avenue of living and providing for my family. The previous travel agency job already had been given away. No other opportunities existed to allow my family and me to remain in that favorite city of mine, where I was born: Madras, where I survived many a twist of life. Now I wondered if I had to go to temporarily settle down in another city? Yes was the answer, and Minnie and I wrapped our few belongings and moved two hundred miles away, to a beautiful city called Bangalore!

In a new city with no place to go to call our abode, Minnie and I along with our first child, now five years old, filled with sadness due

Rev. Paul Kumar

to a foolish mistake, stayed in a hotel temporarily. We went to our old ways once again, with limited funds on hand, unable to pay for the accommodations and eat. We survived with one meal a day, even for our growing child, Victor, and with him at this juncture, my wife was carrying a child, which would be our second. Minnie was very weak and not too healthy after the upheaval of emotions' ebb and tide in regard to our visas, and then my foolishness to abandon the job I had so firmly. Somehow at this time, in this new city, Bangalore, the time was close at hand for the baby to be born. We were unable to be in touch with a gynecologist, until one lady was kind enough to accept Minnie as her patient. Minnie in her time of pregnancy did not have any scheduled doctor's visits, checkups, and no health insurance benefits from employers in India; our only recourse was limited to rushing to local government-run hospitals for all ailments, standing in long lines, awaiting our turn to be seen by a doctor, and being content if we saw one, not thinking of the cure. Now in this strange city, this lady doctor had a small nursing home attached. I knocked on the doors of many travel agencies in the new city until one day, once again, I was blessed with an offer to work, as I candidly advised the owner of my temporary status, awaiting to move on, away, far away, to America! There is always a bridge to cross over to the safer side, for God provides it. Once again His love bridged our lives to meet the immediate needs of a place to stay, and to ensure Minnie's immediate care and concerns for her pregnancy and the safe birth of our next child. We moved from our cheap motel to a two-room tenement that was owned by an elderly lady. Have there been as many red-letter days in your life as there have in mine? Surely I've had my share of them, and one of those was August 4, 1974, in this new city of Bangalore. It was nearly time for my wife to deliver our second child. With the lack of proper nutrition and prenatal care, this newfound lady doctor spoke candidly of her professional concerns and that she could not accept the responsibility of the safe birth of the child, or the trauma to the mother, due to medical reasons at this stage of pregnancy. She spoke of her concerns that the mother or baby could be lost while in delivery. A Sunday afternoon, August 4, 1974, brought uncertainty to an otherwise happy family anticipating going away to a land called America! We were quivering as the day progressed—a Sunday, the Lord's day, the Sabbath, as people went to their houses of worship with church bells ringing melodiously. Deep within my innermost soul, my utterances were, "God, please watch over my love, my wife, and the new life that you have created within her." If I had taken the doctor's words to heart, I would have crumbled to pieces, considering who among the two, mother or baby, would live to see a brand-new world, the land that welcomes all to it's shores, the United States of America, touched by God's rich, heavenly grace and watched over by that same heavenly grace over the ages. "For God shed His grace on thee! America the beautiful!" That Sunday, August 4, 1974, was truly the longest day, when hours and minutes crept ever so slowly, and in the quiet surroundings with hushed silence of a clean nursing home, the strong odor of the fluid "Detol," the antiseptic cleanser, was overpowering, making me very sick too. I continued to pray for mother and baby, resigned to accept God's gift that day; yet with the strong love that drew Minnie and I to be at this point in our lives, I begged God to save her. Mother or baby was the immediate question, when I suddenly began humming slowly a great hymn of the ages by Thomas O. Chisolm: "Great is thy faithfulness, O God my father. There is no shadow of turning with thee. Thou changest not. Thy compassions they fail not. As thou has been, Thou forever will be!" God was truly present in that less modern nursing home, in that labor/delivery room, with just the two women, the lady doctor and my wife in uncontrollable pain, when the nurse advised me to return around 4 p.m. and not to wait for many long hours. Wild, fearful thoughts flooded my inner being, and I nervously chewed my fingernails off their fingers and my heavy footsteps dragged on the hot roads as I thought of life and all of the beauty of togetherness—a family. I also thought of the greater things that God desired to happen that would be lost in a flash of the doctor's scalpel to cut the umbilical cord, and I wondered whose life would be saved. The clock struck 4 p.m. and I was there in the hallways of the nursing home. The entire staff greeted me with genuine smiles of relief

Rev. Paul Kumar

and joy. I knew for sure then that my little baby girl's life's awakening moment had begun with her precious, beautiful mother by her side, clutching her with unconditional love. "But the loving kindness of the Lord is from everlasting to everlasting, to those who reverence him. His salvation is to children's children of those who are faithful to his covenant and remember to obey him" (Psalm 103:17)

LIFE'S DREAM
CAME TRUE

IT WAS EXCITING TO HOLD MY NEWBORN baby girl, the gift that God gave us. She was tiny, with big, expressive eyes, and not much flesh on her bones, just those eyes that jumped up in return to speak and say proudly, "I am alive!" Now we had become a family of four, and the visas were to be issued around January of 1975 by the U.S. Consulate in Madras, the town that we had left. We lived in Bangalore now. Certain that our travel was set for February 1975, Minnie and I had so much to overcome in our financial commitments, such as paying rent for our two-room tenement home, the nursing home bills, and the newborn baby's needs. We did overcome and went back to Madras to obtain our visas and to have the interviews with the U.S. Consulate. Our airline tickets were ready for us to leave from Bangalore, as we planned to leave India for good. The day was February 15, 1975, and we boarded an Indian Airlines jet for the domestic trip from Bangalore to Bombay. From there we boarded a large jet on Swiss Air to Zurich, connecting further from Zurich to the New York (J.F.K.) airport. At the airport, the two adults exchanged Indian rupees to U.S. dollars and they were worth only six dollars. The plane taxied on the runaway and then rose quickly to an altitude of about thirty thousand feet. Looking down below at the dotted landscape—UP, UP, and away we went. We were nearer to the heavens, with puffy white clouds passing by our windows, reminding us of what it would feel to be free. Free from the bonds of cultural restraints, inhibitions that bind and restrict family love, and more. Two lovers, brave as man and wife, accepted all the hard knocks of life, when deep scars were inflicted as people fulfilled their roles, even in close-knit families like Minnie's. Our two children were truly God's gift to help us understand our responsibilities, their innocence, and the purity their future entirely in our hands—a future that now awaited us: America under God's watchful eyes, the envy of the rest of the world. God had his plans to shape and mould in us in a totally new setting, for God alone knows the future ahead for us. "Before I formed you in the womb, I knew you before you were born, I sanctified you (set you apart) and I ordained you a prophet (spokesperson) to the nations" (Jeremiah 1:5). The luxury jetliner sped on its course, crossing oceans and continents and mountain peaks—from golden rays of the sun to the blackness of nights, the dream closer each moment!

While looking out the window of our huge silver bird, man's modern technological achievement, she was descending gradually, as we could see New York's skyline in the distance, and the towering image of the Statue of Liberty, shining in like a beacon of hope. There was snow on the ground, snow on rooftops, and the blend of glass and steel cast beams of light reflective of the early evening sun. In India, in most parts of the land we do not see snow at all. The snow falls in the extreme north of India, atop the mountains of Everest, in the area known as Kashmir. Having lived in the deep southern tip of India, we basically have two seasons: summer and the monsoons, and no winters at all! Minnie and I were improperly dressed for this chilly welcome to the gateway for millions who have passed that way at John F. Kennedy Airport in New York City. Clutching each other, mother, father, a five-year-old, and an infant tiny clinging to dear mother, our feet were now firmly on U.S. soil. Deplaning, we were led to the customs and immigration areas, where officers looked at our passports, and then handed over to us a large brown envelope that was unsealed and that contained our permanent-residence green cards!

Right there, tears of joy and disbelief intermixed streamed down our faces because we were in a land all alone, and were culturally so different. The children were exhausted, the infant was crying to be fed, and Minnie and I were exhausted after long hours of jet travel. After all the entry formalities were completed with the authorities, we were to connect a domestic flight to Atlanta, Georgia, the point closest to Hayesville, North Carolina. The rest of the trip would be made by car. Once again on board an Eastern Airlines flight (then a functioning airline) we felt very much alone, scared, naively praying for God to help us, for it was His plans that enabled our life's dream come true that day! I did remember God's word: "When you pass through the waters, I will be with you, and through the rivers, they shall not overflow you. When you walk through the fire, you shall not be burned, nor shall the flame scorch you. For I am the Lord your God, the Holy one of Israel, your Savior" (Isaiah 43:2-3). Heavenly guidance was the only surety we had. In my head, the knowledge and awareness of scripture, the Bible, came as an assurance: "God is faithful by whom you were called, into the fellowship of His son Jesus Christ, our Lord" (1 Corinthians 1:9). Minnie, on the other hand, true to every emotion and feeling, sure that love still bewildered her personal faith, had walked thus far through each door of opportunity, from the shores of India to the land that beckons the tired and the weary and the burdened to its shores. On arrival in Atlanta, Georgia, we hoped to find the casual friend who had come my way in Bangalore, India, at the travel agency, as I shared the tale of my anticipated travel into Atlanta, prior to going to Hayesville, North Carolina. This friend had settled down in Atlanta, Georgia, and worked for Coca-Cola for many years. On hearing of my prospective future, this friend volunteered to come and meet us at the Atlanta airport. Once we had landed in Atlanta, we were so happy to see my friend and his wife waiting for us at the baggage claim area. We waited for our suitcases to show up on the bag carousel, and suddenly

Rev. Paul Kumar

felt ashamed, for among the suitcases ours was bound with a coil of rope around it, lacking proper locks. Also the contents had spilled out and one could see our undergarments going round and round in front of our friends and other passengers. Hiding our shame, we quickly picked up the loose items and grabbed the torn suitcase out of the carousel before it could split apart. The itinerary and instructions from my employer, were that we check in to our hotel, the Holiday Inn at the airport. The next morning one of his workers would drive from Hayesville to Atlanta and take us back in his car. Our friends now with us agreed to drive us to the Holiday Inn and check us in for the night. On arrival at the hotel, the front desk asked me to pay for the overnight stay. We were led to believe that the accommodations were prepaid by my employer. Minnie and I were penniless, as the currency exchange was just six dollars per adult, and all that was spent in the transit lounge at Zurich, Switzerland. Our kind friends who came to receive us saw our distress and agreed to charge it to a credit card of theirs. Once our accommodations were paid for the night, our friends invited us to go with them to their apartment and have a meal to refresh ourselves and the children. The wife had cooked a good Indian meal, cuisine like that of way back home, in the heart of Atlanta. Curiosity took hold of me, as I had never ever in my life seen living spaces with wall-to-wall carpeting, for in India it is a bare cement flooring, even with the rich. Then my eyes caught a glimpse of the color-coordinated telephones in each room, in 1975, much before the marvel of cell phones. Another marvel was there in a corner of the living area: a huge analog Zenith color television, unlike the technology of today, with high-definition, plasma, and liquid crystal display (LCD) screens. Modern, stainless-steel cooking utensils lined their kitchen, and the wonder of a refrigerator with an ice maker. I knew of an old ice box. Oh! We quickly thought of our first day in our marriage, when Minnie was given a bare earthenware mud pot, a mud oven, a few sticks of firewood, and a cup of rice to boil with water as our meal for the day.

Our friends had adapted very well, enjoying the goodness of this land America and working for the world's largest soft-drink maker,

Coca-Cola, which brought their lifestyle to a high standard. Minnie and I, after a good shower, with our children were ready for the gourmet cooking of Indian cuisine. The table was laid out beautifully with modern chinaware, cutlery, and long-stemmed crystal glasses for a drink of water. The tablecloth was pretty, and after dinner the pleasantries exchanged with our friends were truly kind and made us feel welcome, which otherwise would have turned disastrous. Thus, as dumbstruck as we were to look at the greatness of modern America, God always prepares ahead to carry His plans for His people, once he sets it in motion. Truly "he (God) has brought us to this place, and has given this land (in our case, America), a land flowing with milk and honey" (Deuteronomy 26:9). At a moment and time when we, Minnie and I, a five-year-old, and an infant baby, could have been stranded in a strange city, Atlanta, and to add to that the lack of prepaid hotel accommodations, which was overcome by our friends, they truly cared for us in that short time as family! Scripture speaks again: " There are friends who pretend to be friends,but there is a friend who sticks closer than a brother" (Proverbs 18:24). I now can understand when faith-loving people say, "Those who love the Lord love the people, and God's people are like family, 'the family of God.'" Our newfound friends drove us back to the Holiday Inn for the night, wishing the best for our future.

Hayesville, North Carolina, is a small town nestled in the surroundings of the Blue Ridge Mountains from North Georgia to just across scenic Helen and Hiawassee, overlooking Lake Chatuge, the boundaries of western North Carolina. In Hayesville, many homes are on the banks of the lake, and speed boats with outboard motors purr loudly in the waters of the lake. Our heartbeats were racing above their normal steady beats, for excitement and tiredness combined made us lay our weary heads on the soft, clean, crisp pillows, comfortable sheets, and wide bed at the hotel. We had never slept upon as nice as these before, compared to the cold, bare cement floor in India. We truly could not go to sleep, for the anticipation was great before sunrise, and we were aware that we were so close to "life's dream to come true." In the dark of the night, Minnie and the children were very comfortably at rest, fast asleep, and their faces were so much at ease as the moonlight spread as ribbons the glow through the hotel room windows, causing a glow of God's embracing love for them, and their response was a twitch of a smile parked on their lips.

It made me humble to see such perseverance in Minnie, my wife, the mother with a strong will, a flaming heart, and with burning love for her husband, trusting her life in his hands, as the moon cast shadows of hope and promise from darkness to light. God's word is: "No longer will you need the sun, or moon to give you light for the Lord God will be your everlasting light, and He will be your glory" (Isaiah 60:19). In the stillness and quiet of the night, I thought of how we would by car travel to Hayesville, North Carolina, and about the person who was going to come to pick us up. The early morning sun slowly shed its faint beams to say, "Rise up, the day is at hand." I was restless with concern for the immediate moment about how to provide breakfast and have our infant baby's milk provided. I had no money, nor could I charge it to the room, for nothing was prepaid by the employer. The very thought of the previous evening at check-in to the hotel was a sad reminder of our helplessness. Once again I looked at the beautiful faces of my wife, my boy, and the infant girl with her doe eyes. Her life was given by God to live for a purpose; today she is a mother of two precious kids. Tears brimmed in my eyes, standing helpless to provide the morning toast, coffee, and baby's milk to tide us over for that car trip to Hayesville, North Carolina, 300 miles away. I stared at that well-printed menu card on the table in the room, which excited my taste buds, while my parched lips longed for a hot pot of coffee that was an inborn habit from early days of my life. Everything was far out of reach except the faint sounds of the air-conditioning in the room, like a strange intruder watching our predicament. With a lonesome feeling, I got up the courage to buzz for room service, and soon, as courtesy prevailed, this smiling waiter knocked at our door. Obviously I had no funds to place an order for breakfast, but I in some naive way was able to express my awkward situation, that I needed help. The waiter scanned our room with his eyes, and feelings of pity, concern, and compassion gushed into his inner being. With his kind words, not of ridicule, promised us a breakfast tray from his very own entitlement, to help us with our needs of the moment. Our chaperone to drive us into Hayesville had yet to arrive at the hotel's front desk to enquire about us. That breakfast coffee was sweetened with more than a spoonful of sugar, with granules of God's love stirred into it, allowing that waiter to be our immediate messenger from God. As my family enjoyed their breakfast with much relief, I walked up to the front desk to enquire if someone had come asking about us. "Yes, indeed," the front desk clerk exclaimed, for they advised this man who came to pick us up that we were not registered at their hotel nor had we checked in. "Ouch!" What folly, for the bird at hand was allowed to fly away as I stood with that very deep, sinking feeling of being lost, marooned, having come halfway across the world and now unable to reach the shore, instead being tossed about by uncontrollable elements. My legs weakened as I began to walk down toward our hotel room, with no bright ideas lighting up in my head. I did not know the name of the man who had been sent by our benefactor, my employer, and who had been sent away because of the inept care of the front desk clerk. Many questions rushed to my mind as I sat in our room, while the family was all dressed up, ready to make the road trip to Hayesville, North Carolina. Suddenly there was a knock at our door, and there stood a clean-shaven, middle-aged, well-mannered white male with a well-tailored suit and shiny brown shoes all laced up. He was smartly dressed for the occasion. The man, somehow uncertain of our arrival at the hotel, went to the airport to the airline desk to enquire about a passenger list of the previous evening's Eastern Airlines flight to Atlanta from New York (JFK) and found our names as those on board that particular flight. That brought him back to the hotel, and this time, the clerk directed him correctly to our room. All set to go! This gentleman took our not-so-impressive suitcases, which were half torn, wound with cords, and not Samonsites on wheels, and loaded them into the trunk of a shiny Buick Lasabre sedan with white interior, his proud automobile. Off we went on those

Rev. Paul Kumar

busy interstates of Atlanta, toward North Carolina approximately 300 miles away, for a trip that at a normal speed would be completed in about three and half hours. The skyline of Atlanta sped by and the success stories of large corporations, factories, and showrooms were a wonder for our eyes to feast upon, the true American enterprise. On our way, at the midpoint of our journey on the road, our new friend stopped at a fast-food place (now we know) a Burger King, introducing us for the first time in our lives to the taste of a hamburger with french fries, and a rich vanilla milk shake to drink. "French fries": a lot of long sticks of potatoes fried deep in cooking oil, crisp, and tasty to accompany a round patty of beef topped with a slice of red tomato, and green leaves called lettuce. The beef patty was unknown to Minnie, for in her heritage with Hinduism the cow is a sacred animal that Hindus deeply revere and worship, and they will neither hurt nor kill a cow! Looking back now on that moment in her life, she laughs and jokingly speaks of her choice in eating meats as one who believes that the cow is not to be worshipped, for it is just an animal that God created, as are others.

As our luxury Buick sedan sped from city skylines to rural landscapes with stretches of lush green acres of grass and cattle grazing peacefully with no rush to their lives, to us in the car, rushing toward our destination, the city upon a hill was shining like a beacon of light with the hope and promise for this family of four, now oceans away from their homeland, India! The light shone in spite of times of despair, disappointments, mishaps, and doubts that rose to heights that could have easily dwarfed the light of such hope. What a miracle! Miracles are wrought by God and God alone. In modern society today, we often discount the providential help in miracles that turn people's lives completely. We are able to truly testify to such miracles, and that is why these illustrations are described so vividly, that one may place faith, trust, and hope, and believe! My faith still dangled in my own humanistic thoughts, as my mother was a faithful Christian and so was I, and I would be eligible to enter heaven because of that privilege. What a wrong perception of faith in Jesus Christ! Jesus spoke to His disciples, "'Where is your faith?' They were afraid and marveled saying to one another, 'Who can this be? For He commands even the winds and the water, and they obey Him'" (Luke 8:25). There was not much conversation as the roads were winding over the mountainous section of the Blue Ridge Mountains; he must have wondered within himself if people from a new country with brown complexion and jet-black hair on their heads were the first of their kind to step into Hayesville, North Carolina, a quiet farming town of five thousand inhabitants, by early 1975 estimates. Not now, of course! The drive was smooth, the baby slept peacefully, the boy was fine, Minnie was engulfed in shyness, still clad in her sari; and I looked all around, capturing the serene images of picturesque open fields, farms with horses and cattle grazing, quiet roadways with an occasional car passing through, driveways, and roads dotted with splotches of white snow, unevenly spread over the rich landscape of Hayesville, part of western north Carolina. God's creation was best portrayed with the snow-capped Blue Ridge Mountains in the distance. We were just about to enter the gateway into Hayesville on February 15, 1975, yet another eventful Sunday to note! God's creation was so vivid before our eyes, yet there was no rush in our hearts to have that personal relationship with Him. All head knowledge in me of a wonderful God, and in Minnie's, was not much to think about—just follow the leader! The calling, "Come now and let us reason together, says the Lord, though your sins are like scarlet, they shall be as white as snow" (Isaiah 1:18). How symbolic, and true, that many go to church on a Sunday like that of February 15, 1975, to be able to profess their faith in Jesus Christ and start a personal walk with Him as their Savior! Entering the main highway into the town Hayesville, North Carolina, was no exception. It was a small town with people who professed their Christian faith, attended their churches faithfully, and shared God's love with their neighbors and their own families diligently. Through the car windows as we were entering Hayesville, we saw the simple architecture of the churches, with their tall steeples and the bells tolling as in picture postcards. Church services were in progress, the faithful idle and the many colorful automobiles lined up in rows outside. God truly must have hurt in His heart to observe our non-caring attitudes toward Him, minding our immediate business selfishly. A moment to flashback to talk about God's unwavering faithfulness and love so dear, from that moment when a letter arrived in India at the travel agency in the year 1972 through three long years of waiting for the visas to travel to the U.S.A., and in between the events of life and death from Minnie's pregnancy and our baby girl Monisha's birth. We still did not grasp the goodness and thought maybe it was normal for God to perform miracles upon people. How misconstrued we were in our human thinking! God spoke in His word:

You shall love the Lord your God with all your heart, with all your soul, and with all your might, and these words which I command you today, shall be in your heart. You shall teach them diligently to your children, and shall talk to them, when you sit in your house, when you walk by the way, when you lie down, and when you rise up. (Deuteronomy 6:5-7)

God's candid instructions, strong advice, and strict directive are what He wanted us to grasp, and not to forget the benefits that only He could and did accomplish for us in this land. To this day God truly does, as we much later grasped the essence of His concern over Minnie and I, walking spiritually unconcerned—almost dead! I will not attribute all of this story to fate, or per chance to luck, for there are no such realities! Scripture defines miracles and makes us aware of them to recognize and accept the truth: that there is a God, creator of heaven and earth and all therein.

For the Lord your God is bringing you into a good land, a land of brooks of water, of fountains and springs, that flow out of valleys and hills, a land in which you will eat bread without scarcity, in which you lack nothing, when you have eaten and are full, then you shall bless the Lord your God, for the good land, which He has given you. (Deuteronomy 8:7, 9 and 10)

America the Beautiful, February 15, 1975, when in the bigness of life, life's dream came true.

LIFE'S DREAM
IN MOTION

CHURCH BELLS RANG loudly on that life-changing date of Sunday, February 15, 1975, as God set into motion all of His plans as He desired them to be. After all, it started as a dream in our hearts as we began the journey over a span of three years, 1972 to 1975. We were less enthusiastic as well, blaming governments, policies, and procedures, without totally relying on God, who mastered the plan in the first place and who picked us two very diverse souls, a man of sound Christian head knowledge and a woman, his wife, who faithfully worshipped clay idols of Hinduism as her faith!

The favorite hymn that we often sang in our churches was "To God Be the Glory, Great Things He Has Done." The words of beloved Fanny Crosby. "Praise the Lord, praise the Lord, let the earth hear His voice. Give Him the glory, great things He has done ..." The bells tolled from those church steeples, welcoming us to Hayesville, North Carolina. Our hearts stirred with emotions and tears at to the patriotic refrain, "God Bless America, land that I love." To this very day it is our honest refrain! Three decades later we have never ever lost our gratitude for this land, as we sing "from the mountains, to the prairie, to the oceans white with foam, God bless America, my home sweet home!"

We were winding our way to a lonesome road, where we were to live temporarily in a house rented by the travel agency, a lakeside cabin that otherwise was rented to tourists in the peak summer season, and now was an empty chalet or cabin in the winter and unoccupied. We were to stay till the spring in early April in this part of western North Carolina. We arrived at our cabin's door, and our kind, patient friend and guide let us in to survey our new surroundings. It was about midday in Hayesville, around 1 p.m. local time, cloudy with a dark, overcast snow on the ground, and the cold of the outside we felt inside too. The utilities were all turned on and ready, while we thanked our friend and guide, who we were bound to see more of, and said good bye! Now came the strange, foolish part of not having asked our guide to turn on the floorboard heaters, which were so good to look at, but we could not understand the controls or how to operate them. We looked around at our new home, the cabin meant for tourists; we saw the kitchen area, and in the tradition of American love and generosity, caring and sharing being vital, we saw bags of good grocery items, fresh vegetables, baby food, formula, and diapers.

Where do we begin was the big question. As we stared at the electric stove, we saw the controls marked for each burner: "HI," "LO," and "OFF." Never did it help us to know that it was High and Low stove settings while cooking, relative to each range burner. On a Sunday, all alone in that cabin, we dared not knock on any door, and with no transportation of our own, we could go no farther. Do we starve till someone comes around to enquire about how we are settled in, and help us out in understanding the modern ways of cooking, far from that infamous mud pot with a brick stove and sticks of firewood that cooked our one meal a day in India? How do we keep ourselves warm in that cabin, when we felt the chill within from the cold outside, our cabin overlooking a lake as well? Afraid of doing something wrong, and to avoid any accidents, especially with electric appliances, we decided to best use our body warmth by clinging to each other on the bed already there in the cabin. Well, we saw a shiny colorful tin can of coffee on the kitchen counter. Ah! The aroma of fresh-brewed coffee would be nice on a cold day. After so much of vain emotional excitement, much in wonderment of the things around us, we reached out for that can of Folgers coffee, opened the top, and suddenly saw a tight seal of foil that needed a can opener in order to cut it out. Well, there was an electric can opener left for us; staring at it, we had no clue how to operate it! We left that Folgers coffee can as a showpiece for the time being. Hopelessly lost with no knowledge of how to operate modern gadgets, we checked our wristwatches and knew of the time, which read 10 p.m., in contrast to around 2 p.m. local time in Hayesville, North Carolina, on that Sunday afternoon. Our watches were reading the time in India, for we never understood the changes in time zones across continents. We truly were far behind in our habits; from native India to modern America, in a very progressive world, our thoughts and actions were engulfed in a cultural shock, unable to use the best of the goods to start our lives! Rather take chances, to venture and learn, we decided to forgo many a pleasure. We were shy, hesitant to ask for help from the local Department of Social Services in the county. Monday was around the corner and we decided to wait it out, with no heat and no proper meals, and again, looking at the time on our wrists, we decided that it was bedtime at 10 p.m., unaware of the gulf of difference between the actual time of 2 p.m. outside our doors. We decided to sleep with the cold air within the cabin, unable to turn on the heat from the floorboard heaters that intimidated us. We felt secure to cuddle up together and disperse our own body heat between us.

There must have been a smile and a nod of the head from God in heaven, wondering what more could He do for us? His encouragement came in the form of scripture: "So shall you rejoice in every good thing, which the Lord, your God has given to you, and the Levite, and the stranger, who is among you" (Deuteronomy 26:11). Yes, God has placed us among His people and the stranger employer and benefactor. whose heart was stirred and whom God appointed to carry forth heaven's desire to our betterment in life! We stepped onto the stairway of God's love that seemed to go almost to the heights of heaven; still in comparison, to us, we were allowed to experience heaven on earth with a brand-new way of life in a blessed land called America. As we tossed in our bed, looking toward the two children, the boy, five years old, and the infant girl, now eighteen months, were spared from our cares, concerns, and burdens as they slept peacefully. Outside our bedroom window, we were kept awake by the sounds of cars and loud conversations, much in contrast to our thinking, because of our wristwatches that read Indian time as midnight now! The activity was reasonable and understandable, for the time outside was mid-afternoon on a grand Sunday afternoon like any other, when people after church were in their cars heading home, having conversations with neighbors of sweet visits and fellowship. In India, we never were privy to such extended activities that formed sweet relationships, except for families that confined and locked themselves and their own kin behind closed doors. Dreams were now in motion, and God wanted us to understand and realize that this eventful Sunday, February 15, 1975, was just the start. "For your word's sake and according to your own heart you have done all these great things, to make your servant know them" (2 Samuel 7:21). Having drifted into a sleep for a few hours, startled I woke up to see my watch with Indian time, now reading 5 a.m., and saw darkness outside. The quiet stillness, a starless sky, and the fearful quiet around the cabin, with the lake waters moving, and the sounds of the ripples was eerie. The actual time in Hayesville was around 11 p.m. Sunday night, which accounted for such quietness. Still I was so foolish in reckoning that my wristwatch was deceiving me with a different time and that I needed to synchronize it with the time zone here in the U.S. I was out of sync with everything, including time! And here I was wrapped up in my own ignorance, getting ready to go to work, my grand entrance of my first day at the travel agency. The agency was located in the downtown district of Hayesville, and our lakeside cabin was a few miles away. With small employers, many people went to work in their own automobiles. I had to depend on my employer to pay for my transportation, to and from work, by sending our friend, the guide who brought us from the airport to help.

I was drawn once again to the ugly past, where with inescapable poverty, for an average person like me, I could not have afforded to travel even in a taxi cab. It would have been a high form of luxury. Finally the true dawn in Hayesville, with the glow of a stubborn sun peeping through the gray clouds of a snowy day ahead that spoke of God's faithfulness to me. "And He shall be like the light of the morning, when the sun rises, a morning without clouds, like the tender grass springing out of the earth, by clear shining after the rain" (2 Samuel 23:4). How very true and symbolic of the ground after the purity of the snowfall the previous day, Sunday; and now the early morning sun melting the snow into droplets of water that were like jewels glistening and dotting the lush landscapes of this town, Hayesville, another corner in God's broad landscape of earth!

Ah! My ride came with cheery morning greetings to me and to Minnie, who was left alone with the two small children. She had no one to talk to and was unable to carry on a day's work with all the tasks. She also was unable to operate the cooking stove or make coffee, for the attractive coffee can could not be opened with the electric can opener, as she did not know how to! With no time to attend to small things, I went away to the agency, a new day, a milestone in my travel career. As I walked in, the door mat of welcome was laid out along with the smiling faces of the travel agents, young women from the area who, after completing high school, set out to work. All of them had skills in secretarial and typing work, with my employer and benefactor as owner, well qualified to oversee and run the operation day to day. The agency sat in an area near quiet residential streets, in a neat round house, literally, with picture windows all around; it truly was a landmark for the people in Hayesville and the neighboring towns of Murphy and Andrews, North Carolina, and let's not forget Hiawassee, Georgia. Business was thriving, for people came making their travel plans, as this was the only travel agency in a radius of about 150 miles; the next nearest was in Asheville, North Carolina. I was taken to my

Rev. Paul Kumar

desk that proudly had my name on it, with lots of travel literature and magazines at the side. The day began well, as the next part involved equipping me, I was told. I was to learn driving from my guide every working day, after working hours, in order to be qualified to drive on my own. Strangely it was from employer's antique car collection I was to use a 1956 Studebaker with the front grille resembling that of an airplane nose cone, and with a manual shifter.

"For the Lord God is a sun and shield, the Lord will give grace and glory, no good thing will He withhold, from those who walk uprightly" (Psalm 84:11). For every good that has been given to us, God only wanted our faithfulness, for Minnie and I know Him more personally.

There was that constant tugging at my heart, that with all the head knowledge, and being labeled a "Christian," I needed to go beyond in recognizing and accepting the Good News that Christ died to save me. The apostle Paul was brought to his knees to realize who Jesus Christ was, and the saving grace from heaven was for Paul to say, "For I am not ashamed of this good news about Christ. It is God's powerful method of bringing all who believe it, to heaven. This message was preached first to Jews alone, but now everyone is invited to come to God (including me) in the same way" (Romans 1:16).

The message was simple for me: to accept the Good News that God equips us and makes us ready for heaven after mortal death; to be right, in God's sight, as we place our faith and trust in Christ to save us. From start to finish, scripture says, "The man who finds life will find it through trusting God" (Romans 1:17). God desired that we capture the power of His working in our lives, and wonder why it was measured by any standards of the world, by a man or a woman, walking amid throngs of people in India trying to experience miracles! "For I am offering you my deliverance, not in the distant future but right now. I am ready to save you, and I will restore Jerusalem and Israel who is my glory" (Isaiah 46:13). Am I ready? Is Minnie ready, she who never knew of God as heavenly Father, His son Jesus Christ, the cross, the victory over the grave, His resurrection, his redemption, or the hope for heaven in eternity after mortal death? We both seemed to be struggling along in no rush, avoiding serious thoughts. After the day's hard work, back at my lakeside cabin, I saw the glow in my wife's eyes. She, the strong tower of caring, was given an education about how to operate every appliance, and much more, by the social worker from the Department of Social Services. The freshness of every cup from our Folgers coffee tin was finally unlocked with the help of the can opener, and the brew was inviting. Life moved with a sense of normalcy and restored confidence amid strange surroundings, and our watches were reset to the local time in Hayesville, North Carolina, so we would avoid misreading the time! Unlike India, which had only a few working airlines and a few, limited ways for travel business, here there were ample opportunities to be productive and to bring forth revenue for the travel agency. Time moved ever so quickly, and six months had passed. Spring was around the corner, and tourists would come back for those cabins by the lake we were living in as our temporary home. We were thankful each day: "O Lord, what miracles you do, and how deep are your thoughts" (Psalm 92:5). During this time, I was also promoted to be the agency manager, as the former one was to retire, and I settled down away!

The travel agency was staffed with five young women with their teamwork, their knowledge and expertise, their recognition of the faithful patrons and customers who came for their travel plans each time. It was an asset to help bring my managerial duties to the standards for which this travel agency was noted. I could not but say, "It is good to say thank you to the Lord, to sing praises to the God who is above all gods" (Psalms 92:1). God truly made His very presence known to Minnie and me in a very bold way, to the measure of His work and to accomplish His purpose for which we belong to Him, and to seek Him as our only refuge and strength! "For Jehovah (God) is my refuge. How then can evil overtake me, or any plague come near? For He orders His angels to protect you (me) wherever you (I) go. They will steady you with their hands, to keep you from stumbling again the rocks on the trail" (Psalms 91:9-12). So much of the living spoken words of God,

Rev. Paul Kumar

yet how is it that the conviction of my heart did not occur? God was reminding me not to procrastinate in my knowing Him, His son Jesus Christ: "Pay attention Israel (personally for me) for you are my servant, I made you, and I will not forget to help you; I have blotted out your sins, they are gone like morning mist at noon. O! return to me, for I have paid the price to set you free" (Isaiah 44:21-22). How much clearer can God reveal the plan for salvation? Christ is the answer! For Minnie, my beloved wife, now seven years into our marriage, the only reminder and witness was that my Bible was always prominently placed for her to pick up and read, to which she was very faithful, for God allowed her to search within the longings of her heart. She desired to know more. I could not be an effective witness, for I did not know how to express it, other than my own faithfulness to God as a lifestyle. This would open up the pathway to life's dreams in motion, that Minnie and I, each, individually, personally, would profess our true faith in commitment and arrive at one common ground of thinking and acceptance of the truth: that Christ died for our sins, upon a rugged cross, for He loved us first (before we could) and with the faith of a child, we would trust our lives each in God's hands. So many had to accept Christ in that manner.

Trembling with fear, the jailer called for lights and ran to the dungeon, and fell down before Paul and Silas. He brought them out, and begged them, "Sirs, what must I do to be saved?' They in turn replied, "Believe on the Lord Jesus Christ, and you will be saved, and your entire household." (Acts 16:29-31)

Minnie and I were spiritually groping in the dark, asking God to help us. Scripture reaffirms: "Because of His kindness, you have been saved through trusting Christ, and even trusting is not of yourselves. It too is a gift from God. Salvation is not a reward, for the good we have done, so none of us can take any credit for it" (Ephesians 2:8-9). While we are sharing with you so much about our own faith and the lack thereof, what about my employer? The travel agency owner blessed with everything from riches to stature in the town, pride and recognition, prosperity, health and wisdom, and with life large enough to live comfortably? He had a very strange perception of faith, spirituality, and life around it. He refused to accept God as creator of the world, the heavens and the earth, and everything in it. He also did not accept the truth: that God made him in His likeness. It showed of his blindness to the truth. "God has shut their eyes, so that they cannot see, and closed their minds from understanding" (Isaiah 44:18). In spite of the human side of this man, with kindness, tolerance, community outreach, and amicable living amid faith-loving people of the town of Hayesville, all wondered, including Minnie and me. God's words are powerful and go directly to the heart. It is for us to accept or reject. There is that choice. God says, "Let all the world look to me for salvation, for I am God; there is none other. I have sworn by myself and I will never go back on my word, for it is true, that every knee in all the world shall bow to me, and every tongue shall swear allegiance to my name" (Isaiah 45:22-23). My eployer swore no allegiance to divine authority, nor attributed his life and his success to God's provision and help! A time, a situation, and a circumstance came to validate the spiritual visage of this man the travel agency owner with his own agency manager: me! There was an immediate need for payroll checks to be signed by the owner so I could distribute them to the employees. On this day, I drove up a steep driveway in my very own used car, a Dodge Dart, being a good driver by now. This driveway led me up to a modern, mountaintop log cabin nestled among tall, towering trees with birds chirping, singing melodiously. The towering Blue Ridge Mountain peaks in the distance cast a watchful shadow, and the hush of silence away from city sounds, and the puffy white clouds sailing across the Carolina skies where the undoubtable revelation of God and His handiwork. Such a perfect setting formed the modern technological living quarters for this man who would not have any part of God, or faith, not allowing his stubborn heart to grant any credit, yet he lived in and among such unadulterated surroundings without any wonder at all. A sudden stirring sound of motor-driven security cameras at vantage points of that luxury mountaintop cabin alerted me. Then came the flapping sounds of the banner—red, white, and blue, strung on a stately tall flagpole—that testified of at least his patriotic allegiance to the land that welcomed this powerful native Swede to succeed in free enterprise: the U.S.A. Usually it is allegiance of any to God and country; here it was by the view of the flag of the United States fluttering in the wind. Truly, allegiance to his country was validated, but not to God. Stranded atop with all that beauty in God's creation, the marvel of modern technology, and the power of the flag of our nation that welcomes the weary, the lost, and the poor to be free, I stepped up to the door ready to knock and announce my arrival at a time of business! I saw a strange door knocker unlike any other design. I was aghast at the symbolism: the design was the face of a devil with piercing red eyes staring back at me. What kind of a novelty for this luxury log cabin? What could be the connection? Was this a bold statement to anyone from the man behind the closed doors, his personal fascination with the devil, with his belief and convictions in life entrusted to him? I felt unclean at touching that door knocker; there was no doorbell with chimes to alert my boss! It was a very honest reaction to this Christian-raised man, whose mother spoke of the devil and evil, with destruction to one's life even after life ends on earth and languishing in a fiery pit for all eternity! The devil is an enemy to God himself, challenging God's people all the time. I also did remember my mother's advice to stand up bravely when confronted by the devil, and to claim safety by pronouncing the name of Christ aloud with reference to the shed blood of Jesus upon the cross. One never can forget a mother's faithfulness in her upbringing of her child, and many years after her death, this was the required armor to confront evil at this door. "You believe that there is one God. You do well, even the demons believe, and tremble" (James 2:19). The agency owner knew of my arrival; he acted normally and smiled to welcome his manager, whose life-changing moments in the annals of history he had worked so hard to achieve and for which I waited three long years. With a sigh of relief he must have said, "Well done, you gave this family a truly grand future!" I now was in the center of his palatial living quarters, and my eyes wandered with curiosity and intrigue at this man. Once again amid the contemporary decor, I saw an exact replica of the image outside on a door knocker, now three times that size in a glass case enshrined with spotlighting above for accent. Due to my ingrown knowledge of God and scriptures and my awareness of good and evil, angels, and demons, instinctively words came out. Challenging my boss, I said, "Sir, don't you believe in God?" It was a trigger to arouse his anger; with flaming red eyes he looked at me and asked me to leave the premises immediately after he signed the payroll checks.

With the natural blessings that God bestowed upon America, founded with rich, Christian faith and values such as justice, equality, acceptance, came the people of the world to seek solace and refuge, and to enjoy God's blessings. The beauty of nature that encircled Hayesville, North Carolina, failed to bring new life and thinking into this man. Local pastors and loving people withdrew from bringing the truth to him in witness, to trust in an eternal God. Scripture has advice for this man: "Do not love the world, or the things of this world. If anyone loves the world, the love of the Father is not in him, for all that is in the world, the lust of the flesh, the lust of the eyes, and the pride of life is not of the Father, but is of the world" (John 2:15-16). Sound advice for me, my wife, and my children to this day! My family, having come to the greatest nation in the world, could succumb to the dragnet and be drawn into such vanity and pride, thinking that my wife and I could have it all, failing to recognize where it came from. "Praise God from whom all blessings flow!" My departure from his log cabin was a strange mountaintop experience, although I am confident no harm could have come to me, for God watched every moment of my visit there. This employer,my benefactor was an agnostic, and had no desire to change! "For whoever calls upon the name of the Lord shall be saved" (Romans 10:13This man was proud and headstrong! I wondered as I made my way back toward the travel agency, where his eternal rest be? "For the wages of sin is death, but the gift of God is eternal life in Christ Jesus our Lord" (Romans 6:23). With so much of faith, and scripture speaking of God, His son Christ, my wife and I were no different in that we were not surrendering our lives to Christ and were portraying ourselves as better my benefactor, who totally denounced faith and God. All of us have to, once and for all, settle life's eternal rest, for physical death is sure for every human being in this world. Jesus extends an invitation: "I am the Resurrection and the Life. He who believes in me, though he may die, yet he shall live" (John 11:25). The agency staff was not surprised at my observations after that visit to the mountaintop home of my boss. They remarked that for years, the efforts of local clergy, loving people, and friends were fruitless. We continued our work diligently for the purpose of our trusted roles, to promote goodwill, service, caring, and to bring back profits to a successful business in the travel field. We were recognized, and the community accepted Minnie and me, with our two children, embracing them with honest love, caring, and sharing, as most communities do in our precious land. No distinctions were placed upon any one of us, even though we did not look alike, for we came from a land afar, as a part of life's dreams in motion.

The travel agency, having been a welcome business in the community of Hayesville, showed much progress with our personal services we delivered, including airline tickets and travel documents, to residents, our own customers, door to door. My mother always spoke of the faithfulness of Christ to His people, saying, "Jesus never fails." It was driven into me, for she trusted that promise dearly in her heart. It remains always as a sacred memory of her, a truth to hold on to in my life. "For as the rain comes down, and the snow from heaven, and do not return there, but water the earth, and make it bring forth and bud, that it may give seed to the sower" (Isaiah 55:10). I have learned to embrace the old adage, "Treat people with kindness and respect, with honesty, as you would want to be treated yourself." I endeavor to practice such a golden rule each day in my life. "And now abide faith, hope, love; there are three things that remain faith, hope, and love, and the greatest of these is love" (1 Corinthians 13:13). My employer, my benefactor, was not a faith-loving man nor was he a believing Christian. I had to personally be exposed to his convictions; even though they were tragically disappointing, they remained deep and firm in his heart. What are the depths of my convictions, and that of my beloved wife, whose worldly convictions were equal to that of one giving her life, to bring forth joy to another? She did all that for the sake of falling in love. She sacrificed much, yet had she reckoned her personal faith and belief apart from her worldly husband and her two precious children, later to be three, in her life? "But these are written that you may believe that Jesus is the Christ, the son of God, and that believing you may have life in His name" (John 20:31). Faith has content and is of priceless value to a person. Faith leads to eternal life in a believer. Just the namesake of Christianity is not enough, nor can a son dedicated to a faithful Christian mother, claiming family relationship, able to reach heaven's door. "Most assuredly I say unto you, He who hears my word, and believes in Him who sent me, has everlasting Life" (John 5:24). You now know Minnie, the most beautiful woman I fell in love with, and her steadfast, unfailing love holding me and our children, still went through the ebb and flow of her troubled heart with emotions, trying to choose her eternal destiny and settle the issue once and for all. Living every moment with me exposed to prayer and reading the Bible with it, her inner peace was made stronger and the desires of her heart gained purpose but lacked her confession: in whom would she believe? "But if we confess our sins to Him, He can be depended upon, to forgive us, and to cleanse us from every wrong" (1 John 1:9). Christ died for our sins to do this for us.

The community of Hayesville expressed God's love to us and reminded us of the lessons of sharing, which we never could learn in India. In a poverty-stricken home such as mine, there was nothing left to share. What would I know of sharing and the very blessedness in giving? In the home of Minnie, the very rich and proud family had much to offer, but they were selfish and had no concern for anyone outside the house, and lacked reasons and needs for it around their whitewashed bungalow and well-stocked kitchens. Would she have heard about sharing? The people of Hayesville were driven within themselves to reach out and help neighbors, to love them. Minnie and I would find baskets filled with vegetables, corn, and tomatoes from their gardens, and they welcomed us into their modest homes to partake of a friendly meal cooked with love to share. Most of the residents were

Rev. Paul Kumar

"homegrown," generation to generation, and we were not like them yet were no strangers to them. The town had a courthouse on the square; a Western Auto hardware store with a pharmacy and a soda fountain that made delicious malts and shakes; a Family Dollar Store; and the five and ten, as well as the famous Wachovia Bank around the corner. Down the road was a community health center run by the county, where able physicians visited to treat prolonged illnesses in people week after week. There was a county sheriff, with his law-abiding officers, who maintained law and order. The town erected a grand welcome banner in its truest form in action. The turning point for our prolonged desire was in life's dreams in motion toward our personal faith, as our neighbors invited us to worship with them in their churches, unaware of Minnie's and my denominations, and we faithfully attended each Sunday Protestant churches within the community of Hayesville.

We were slowly moving toward the grand day we never knew was forthcoming; not long after our faithfulness in church, God's plans were set to motion for Him to call Minnie and me His very own. Then God desired that we spread the Good News to our children, who are *no* different and not restricted in their freedom to choose their individual faith. As parents we were also entrusted with that responsibility to guide our children in faith as a part of their upbringing. "You shall teach them diligently, to your children, and shall talk of them when you sit in your house, when you walk by the way, when you lie down, and when you rise up" (Deuteronomy 6:7).

"So then faith comes by hearing, and hearing by the word of God" (Romans 10:17). We were well on our way to hearing God's word, not to dream anymore but to act upon them.

LIFE'S FAITH
JOURNEY

MINNIE AND I ARE NOW A FAMILY with three children, with the newest addition, a daughter, Sabrina, born at a very special time in America's history: the bicentennial year, 1976, in Gainesville, Georgia. She truly was, then and now, an added blessing and a proud American-born citizen. In praisescripture reminds me "How precious also are your thoughts to me O God. How great is the sum of them" (Psalm 139:17). The spiritual journey was God's desire, that we draw closer to Him, individually, and be like a family, aware of Jesus Christ and honoring Him in our household as the living God. We have been placed and set in a land that was founded with true respect for God in America! "I am the Lord, and there is no other. There is no God beside me. I will gird you, though you have not known me" (Isaiah 45:5). In our recent visits to churches, where Christ was the foundation and His messages were spoken, we listened with all attentiveness and others in the community watched us to see if we were just going through the motions outwardly or if we were sincere in our longing to confess and profess Christ as Lord of our lives! God was smiling and knew our actions, from deep within, our souls restless and tossed like the waves

Rev. Paul Kumar

at high tide, lashing the shore with an urgency. "Even the spirit of truth, whom the world cannot receive, because it neither sees Him, nor knows Him, but you know Him, for He dwells in you, with you" (John 14:17). Minnie and I needed to confirm that truth and tell others that truly we individually had invited Christ to dwell in our hearts by His Holy Spirit. One eventful Sunday, as usual friends invited us to worship with them. We sat with reverence and listened to a country preacher, who in his distinctive voice, clear and loud, spoke of God's love, His Son Jesus Christ, the death on an old rugged cross, and the victory over death in Christ who rose from the dead and is alive! "For God so loved the world (so loved me) that He gave us His only begotten Son, that whosoever (which includes me and Minnie both) believes in Him, should not perish but have everlasting life" (John 3:16). "To be very true for me to understand (the personal words in italics), to bring me to that reckoning once and for all, Christ died for you, He gave His life for you. Trust in Him," said the preacher, and this seared through my heart, unable to comprehend the magnanimity of such love that no human can ever give. For Minnie, wavering and wandering with an uncertain feeling, this scripture was a reminder: "And you shall know the truth and the truth shall set you free" (John 8:32).

Christ said in His mission: "I have come that they may have Life, and have it more abundantly!" (John 10:10). Abundantly not in worldly fortunes or name, but to be filled with new life, new ways, and new actions in our behavior, for Christ in us ought to be the life we lead, a gift that is defined as an unmerited favor known as <u>GRACE</u>. It was instantaneous and unexpected; that is how God in His Holy Spirit nudges you to proclaim your willingness to allow Christ to come in to your heart. Minnie obeyed instantly, as she stepped out of her seat with renewed courage, a contrite spirit, and brokenness in her heart, and said to the preacher that she needed a Savior, Jesus, to come into her heart and life from that moment on. The picture before us was of a beautiful woman married for seven years, a devoted mother whose entire life centered around worshipping idols, until 1968 and later, staring mutely with no meaning, many of them, in a methodical form of religion.

Worldly riches and pride were added forms of denial to loving others, and now she was emptied of all vanity; instead, she had a truly broken spirit, as though dead in spirit, humbled to accept the truth that before God she was nothing. Minnie needed God's forgiveness of failures and disobediences to Him, and needed to receive restoration and healing of her brokenness by His unending love. Her troubled heart, in not having understood much of scriptures that she would read daily, at that moment must have subdued her with a gentle calm as Jesus spoke silently, "Did I not say to you, that if you would believe, you would see the glory of God?" (John 11:40). There were no outward signs of a breathtaking fashion such as lightning or thunder outside the church walls, nor was the earth moving under our feet; still God's healing of a soul longing for the truth, now received, revived and refreshed her, as she heard softly Christ calling out her name: "Menuka, you are a child of God." That is my way of summing it all up. Scripture again does illustrate an Ethiopian with Phillip who spoke to him of God. The Ethiopian asked of Phillip, "See here is water, what hinders me from being baptized?" For Minnie that would be the next path to take in her life's faith journey. Phillip spoke to the Ethiopian, "If you believe with all your heart, you may." (Minnie did.) The Ethiopian man answered, "I believe that Jesus Christ is the son of God" (Acts 8:37). (So did Minnie.) The wonder is that God touches the yearning soul any time, any place, with no preset plans or fanfare. This little church did not have its own baptismal inside. The joy of being baptized was to be outdoors, in a small creek by the roadside, on a cold March morning in Hayesville, North Carolina. It was to be a day of total freedom from any inhibitions of Minnie's heart.

The day came when Minnie on her own needed a Savior, and in her heart over the span of the seven years of her marriage she had been tossed about with her own confusion about who is her God. She weighed all the truths, from mute clay idols to the statues of the Catholic faith, and then the revelation that God gave His only Son Jesus for her sins and rose again on the third day to give us life, a hope for heaven, when our mortal life ceases on earth. From that

Rev. Paul Kumar

moment until today, when the question is asked what made her seek Christ, she firmly responds, saying, "He is a living Savior, and I serve HIM. There is no other faith where the god they worship has risen from the dead as Christ did. They still remain in their earthly graves, while Christ reigns in heaven seated on a throne, and He will return one day to take His people with Him." This change to Minnie's heart was a total change to her, and she understood that as she had given so much in earthly living to marry me, she now gave up her entire life into the hands of a Savior, Redeemer, and Friend, Jesus Christ. The apostle Paul, who was Saul, gave his life up to Christ and became a warrior for the cause of Christianity. Jesus spoke, "To open their eyes, and to turn from darkness to light, and from the power of Satan to God, that they may receive forgiveness of sins, and an inheritance among those who are sanctified (set apart) by faith in me" (Acts 26:18). Minnie did realize and sought the heavenly light to guide her in life from that moment on!

Minnie in her joys, knowing Christ is her Lord, wondered about my Christian growth, all the while having been the catalyst for her searching scripture, reading much, and desiring to know Jesus Christ to be saved, while I was still wobbling about without a bold profession of my faith in Jesus Christ as my Savior. Scripture reminded me: "Can't you see, that He has been waiting all this time, without punishing you, to give you time to turn from your sin? His kindness is meant to lead you to repentance" (Romans 2:4). Once again the next evening, Minnie and I were in church, as the revival meetings went on into the week. The message was as clear as it was the day before: Jesus died on a cross for your sins; Jesus loves you, and wants you to know Him personally as your Savior. Well, I stared at the preacher and thought, How much more personal can the message be? It was Christ's invitation to me, not the preacher, so I stood up and walked toward the front of the church, asking the preacher to pray, pronouncing my allegiance to the lamb of God, who died for the sins of the world, and also for me!

I was thirty-three years of age, and my confession, asking Jesus Christ to come into my heart and life, erased that home-raised reasoning: that I was born into a Christian family, taught much about the faith by a true, faith-loving, devoted mother, and therefore, I was entitled to a free pass to enter heaven when I died on earth. This was a very wrong notion, a misconception of the very reason why Christ died on a cross and rose again as living proof! I needed to profess Christ as my Savior personally, to take hold of my life, from that day forward, till the days of life's end.

Christ rose from the dead, and will never die again. Death no longer has any power over Him. He died once for all to end sin's power, but now He lives forever in unbroken fellowship with God. So look upon your old Sin nature as dead, and unresponsive to sin, and instead be alive to God, alert to Him, through Jesus Christ our Lord. (Romans 6:9-11)

Sound advice for a man who stagnated in the muddy waters of vain knowledge of the head but not that of the simple reasoning of his heart. Now that stagnant water was made afresh to spring forth anew like a geyser gushing upward!

Minnie and I were to be baptized, as was intended in a roadside creek, on a cold spring day in March. Why be baptized, you ask? Scripture gives the reason as a must:

Your old sin-loving nature was buried with Him (Christ's death on the cross) by baptism, when He died, and when God the Father with glorious power, brought HIM back to Life again (Christ's resurrection), you were given (Minnie and me) His wonderful new life to enjoy. For you have become a part of Him, and so you died with Him, so to speak, when He (Christ) died, and now you share His new life, and shall rise as He did. (Romans 6:4-5, 8)

That very day in the cold creek waters, I felt a strange but sweet release within my heart, as though a big boulder of lies that weighed me down, unable to stand up boldly, was washed away in that flowing current of that stream. Minnie felt the same way; she remarked that when she was immersed in that cold creek and raised up to look unto the heavens, she knew that there was forgiveness, acceptance, belonging (to Christ), and an identity (a child of God). Minnie and I felt as new babies in Christ; yes, new believers, like being born again physically, helpless, needing spiritual milk, and strong meats later to grow strong in Christ. Therefore, laying aside all malice, all guile, hypocrisy, envy, and all evil speaking, as newborn babies desire pure milk of the word that you may grow thereby (1 Peter 2:1-2). Our spiritual journey became personal as "life's faith journey."

Minnie and I continued our lives as normal, except deep within our hearts we both had newfound joy and peace that the world could not. Remember my boss, the travel agency owner,, the instrument God used to bring us over to USA?. He remained adamant in regards to his personal faith as an atheist. While he was in his life of luxury, it was interrupted when he suffered a major heart attack and was sent to the Texas Methodist Hospital in Houston for a heart bypass surgery. Sadly during that procedure on the operating tablemy boss suffered a setback to the extent that he lost the power to speak and to hold with a grip even a pen or anything else in his hands. After the surgery, returning to Hayesville, North Carolina, he was eager to get back to his active business routines, plus running the travel agency. As days went by, frustrations began to discourage him and remind him of the great assets of his being so articulate prior to his surgery, and now the lack of it, also expressed in his writing. Sign language became one possibility for his communication to his employees. Days became long, tired, and wearying, consuming his every strength, for there was no progressive rehabilitation or therapy to follow. With his stately six-foot-three-inch-tall frame my boss made a decision to close down the travel agency business, for it was too much of a burden in the circumstances of that moment. What would be the future of this very noted travel agency? It was a landmark in the heart of Hayesville, a place where unique friendships were made among the average and the wealthy traveler, and it served a lot of towns throughout the stretch of Highway 64 up to Asheville, North Carolina, as well as to Georgia in Hiawassee, Blairsville, and Young Harris. Goodwill and harmony, young and old, came from the students in their high school trips who were now asking these patrons to seek travel agencies in Chattanooga, or Asheville, North

Carolina. A true test of our faith was at the doorstep for Minnie and I. As husband and wife, we became well settled and thought of, and my career with the travel agency was the finale to our road to success. We even took a bold step to own our own FHA-type home, in the heart of Hayesville, so I could walk easily to work each day and come home for lunch. The FHA home brought back memories of the apartment I saw first when we were in Atlanta, where our friends took us to refresh and eat with them. It had wall-to-wall carpeting in the colors of our taste, spacious bathtubs, wall-mounted Trimline phones, and a back porch that brought the Blue Ridge Mountains much closer into view and we could see their changing moods and colors, as humans do so often. It was a dream home, our own, we had wanted for how long now, with the insecurity of the very job that enabled us to own it in the first place? There was another travel agency at least 200 miles away. Once again God's promises, "Casting all your care upon Him, for He cares for you" (1 Peter 5:7).

All travel agencies send their customers on various airlines to get them comfortable with their itineraries. So the major ones, such as United, Delta, American, and the foreign carriers, all play a vital role in the interests of the travel agency, as does the agency to the airlines in turn. Every month the sales representatives of these airlines would pay courtesy visits and enquire about the business turned over to them that formed a certain amount of their credit as revenue. One particular friendship blossomed from the sales manager for United Airlines, as we would turn over considerable revenue to them from travel arrangements made for our customers. "The friendly skies" was the slogan of United Airlines and their friendship played a vital role at this time, when the travel agency was to advise them of our voluntary shutdown due to the failing health of the owner. For Minnie and me, our future seemed crumbling in its infancy, with our stay of two years and six months in this great land, America! The liability of this new home from the FHA administration, with no other means of income and no travel career, for this was the only travel agency in town, brought sadness and disillusionment. The sales representative

Rev. Paul Kumar

from United Airlines, who did not in the least anticipate news of this kind, started his trip from his offices in Chattanooga, Tennessee, and drove miles to visit and enquire about our revenue for the airline he represented. Upon hearing the news, this person suggested that I forward a résumé to the offices of United Airlines in downtown Atlanta, and that his recommendations were available, with many references for the good work I did for the travel agency promoting United Airlines in the market for our revenue. God's intervention was so needed at this time, for no one else could help.

And the Father who knows all hearts, knows of course, what the spirit is saying, as He pleads for us, in harmony with God's will. And we know that all that happens to us, is working for our good, if we love God, and are fitting into His plans. (Romans 8:27-28)

I had no choice to debate within my mind, looking back now. I had learned a valuable lesson: to surrender to God's direction on the next step, and to take us away from the beauty of the Blue Ridge Mountains—with the backdrop of Hayesville, a sweet, loving town that loved God and neighbor—to a big city, making it a part of life's faith journey.

LIFE'S COURSE AND NEW DIRECTION

THE MEMORIES OF HAYESVILLE will always remain in our faithful hearts for the simplicity of true loving of strangers who came into their town and had no jealousies nor any prejudices. They saw we were different, with smooth, brown complexions, black hair adorning our heads, and fluent English with a slight British accent. True, India was, after all, under British rule up until 1947, when there was India's independence. This change over the horizon for us to leave Hayesville, North Carolina, with so much of uncertainty, came so suddenly—as sudden as the reasons that caused it: the heart attack of my benefactor and employer.. Closing down the agency was emotionally so hard for a proud Swede who was welcomed to this land, America, like the millions who also came from distant parts of the world, dreaming of a better tomorrow and a future to build upon. Only America can offer that dream, even today and into the future ahead. Minnie and I could not even dream of such a future, for each day spent in India was focused on that day's survival, dreading the next day and a repeat performance of dreaded poverty.

Rev. Paul Kumar

That was then, 1968-1975, after which the flood gates opened up as heaven smiled upon us to give us miracles and hope, planting us in America the beautiful. God's wonders never cease, yet human doubt causes sadness now such as in life's changing new course and direction!

The hope of a new opportunity in a new city loomed before me as the only ray of hope. My résumé to United Airlines did not even fill up a page with my experience in order to impress them. "'For I know the plans I have for you,' says the Lord, 'they are plans for good and not for evil, to give you a future and a hope'" (Jeremiah 29:11). United Airlines wanted us to appear on a certain date at their local downtown Atlanta offices for an interview. We had caring friends back in Hayesville willing to drive us down to Atlanta. I had not even known how far Atlanta was; the first time, when were brought into Hayesville, we did not observe minute details, for we were excited to see Hayesville. We could only rely on praying for God's grace and direction. "In those days when you pray I will listen. You will find me when you seek me, if you look for me in earnest" (Jeremiah 29:12-13). Minnie and I truly relied on God's plans. As miles rolled by, we were heading toward Atlanta, when suddenly the towering skyscrapers of glass and steel that formed the landscape of Atlanta were in view. I arrived at the lobby of this building: United Airlines Reservation Center. The smiles and courtesy calmed my nervous feelings as I was directed to a room.

The interviews were over and I was told to await a letter from their offices by the following week. "I bless the Holy name of God, with all my heart. Yes I will bless the Lord and not forget the glorious things He has done for me" (Psalms 103:1-2). I was awaiting my interview outcome, which would determine life's new course and direction. I did receive the letter as promised from United Airlines, and I nervously opened the letter only to read kind words of my professionalism, product knowledge, and travel agency expertise, including those of their sales representative from Chattanooga, who was overseeing our travel agency. United Airlines spoke of the competitive nature of the interviews and was unable to give me an opportunity to join them. It was a true disappointment for Minnie and me, and our faithful friends who drove us the distance to downtown Atlanta. "Hear my prayer, O Lord, answer my plea, because you are faithful to your promises" (Psalms 143:1). We were downcast, when the phone rang and was the voice of the officer from Human Resources of United Airlines. He had called to say that their official letter to me was in error and was to be ignored, and that I was to go back to Atlanta for a medical examination to be able to join training classes for the position of a reservation sales agent. The turn of events reassured me "but the eyes of the Lord are watching over those who fear Him, who rely upon His steady Love" (Psalms 33:18-19). God was charting the course to life's new direction, and we were lost with excitement, forgetting the liability of the new FHA home in our hands. The new job was about 300 miles away, and our FHA home could not be sold overnight! With the training in Atlanta, we had to make some serious decisions about how I would be able to complete it; with my family left behind, where would I stay alone for the duration of the training?

Minnie and I were reminded of our one-time causal acquaintances who came to the Atlanta airport and met us the first time we arrived in the U.S. We asked of their help once again, if I could be in their home for the duration of the eight weeks of training. My family would wait for our FHA home on the market to be sold. I was able to come to North Carolina to be with the family, and I admired the courage of Minnie and the children, alone with God's watchful eye over them. Truly, another part of God's plan was directing this course, and the training was over after eight weeks. "Who then can ever keep Christ's love from us? When we have trouble or calamity, when we are hunted down, or destroyed, is it because He doesn't love us anymore? And if we are hungry, or penniless, or in danger or threatened with death, has God deserted us?" (Romans 8:35). What an assurance to hold on to in life!

For I am convinced that nothing can ever separate us from His love, death can't, life can't. The Angels won't and all the powers of Hell itself cannot keep God's Love away. Our fears for today, our worries about tomorrow, or where we are, high above the sky, or in the deepest ocean, nothing will ever be able to separate us from the Love of God, demonstrated by our Lord Jesus Christ, when He died for us. (Romans 8:38-39)

While in training with United Airlines, and commuting on weekends to be with the family in Hayesville, North Carolina, our FHA home was sold, relieving us of that liability, setting us free to make a move to the big city of Atlanta. The memories of Hayesville, North Carolina, can never be erased from the memories of our lives. It was the place that forever changed our life's course and direction from 1975 to 1978, when the pages had to be turned over to a new direction. God's power was the ultimate driving force that gave real meaning to our lives. It was a part of our life's history to tell everyone that my family is a part of the throngs of people from all nations in the world who envy and do their best to come to the greatest nation in the world, one nation under God, called America. On arrival in the big city of Atlanta, Georgia, we had no other choice but to settle down into apartment living, seemingly luxurious to us, and to enjoy the wall-to-wall carpeting, the trimline phones on the wall, the patio, the big bathtubs, and all the amenities that loomed so large! We truly as a family were very grateful for the new opportunities, having received Christ into our hearts. Minnie and I felt our need to grow spiritually, in a church, we could call a part of our life.

We were faithful on Sunday mornings as a family in churches near our apartment complex, which were not far to drive to. The old Dodge Dart was our family car. "God is faithful by whom you were called into the fellowship of His son Jesus Christ our Lord" (1 Corinthians 1:9). Christ was in control of our lives, steering us as a household to life's new direction. We wanted to be a part of a church where we would be able to learn and grow spiritually and serve one another, extending God's love.

And let us consider one another, in order to stir up love and good works, not forsaking the assembly of ourselves together, as is the manner of some, but exhorting one another, and so much more you see the day approaching. (Christ's imminent return). (Hebrews 10:24-25)

A friend of ours recommended that we visit a church about twenty-three miles away from where we lived, to hear a very powerful exposition each Sunday of God's word and His teachings from the Bible in sound doctrine.

We were very eager to go and locate this church, for we were so new to this city and its surroundings. We were able to speak to a person in the church building who welcomed us, trying to help us. We understood from that person of the church its primary purpose of proclaiming Christ to the communities around by a very faithful pastor. "All scripture is given by inspiration of God, and is profitable for doctrine, for reproof, for correction, for instruction in righteousness, that the man of God may be complete, thoroughly equipped for every good work" (2 Timothy 3:16-17). We did make up our minds to be a part of this church and drove each Sunday twenty-three miles each way from where we were in the apartment. It was a blessing to us, for it enabled us to grow with God's grace and knowledge spiritually! In that span of time our children, now three of them, grew up equally in their young minds, as I had been long ago due to my dear faith-loving mother, who insisted that faith be deeply taught and upheld by me. There would be that moment in each child when they too would arrive with that urge, and the recognition that they needed Christ in their lives personally, not to walk around with so much head knowledge of the Bible, scriptures, and of God, like I did for thirty-three years of my life. I then humbled myself to understand that all that knowledge was useful, yet without Christ in my heart life was meaningless. Now I am saved, and am able to guide my children to that awareness through the church. Parental teachings, behavior, and actions matter most to our children, with their young minds, and scripture instructs well. "Run from anything that gives you the evil thoughts, that young men often have, but stay close to anything that makes you want to do right. Have faith and Love, and enjoy the companionship of those who love the Lord, and have pure hearts"

(2 Timothy 2:22). This church was able to meet our spiritual needs, with their caring love, Bible studies, and very articulate exposition of God's word preached by the pastor. Thus, as parents, we in a course of being a part of this church for eleven years saw each of our three children, in their own personal time and space, make their decision for Christ as personal, and accepted God's salvation in their lives! They were also baptized in this church, individually in the course of time, as their public profession of their faith! "Now your attitudes (ours), and thoughts must all be constantly changing for the better. Yes! you must be a new and different person, Holy and good. Clothe yourself with this new nature" (Ephesians 4:23-24). The entire family, now in the very lifestyle of what God desired, entrusting ourselves daily to His direction, felt very stable and wholesome when exposed to the world around us. Here we were in a new city, as big as Atlanta, Georgia, alone with no next of kin, in an apartment living, part of a big church that steered us right spiritually, and I had a stable career with an airline and children in public schools for their education; truly, it was overwhelming

The next course of our life to change was in motion but was already set by God through a person in that big church to which we belonged. He came up and spoke to us, and admired in us the faithfulness of driving twenty-three miles each way for church services. He wondered why we were not keen to move any closer to the church location. He indicated that with three young children, it would be better to own a home rather than rent an apartment, living with lease renewal every year and rent being increased, with no means of ownership at all! Heaven's pulse beats did not rest, and God wanted to fulfill the need in this area of our lives. One Sunday morning this kind person, who cared enough to recommend the need to own a home, came up to me and handed me an envelope. I did not think much of it and attended the church services, and then went back to the apartment. Minnie and I did not feel the urgency to open that envelope, and I almost forgot it in my pocket of the suit I had worn to church! Leisurely we thought of it and opened the envelope only to find a check written to us, from the Merrill Lynch Bank, in the amount of $2,000, with no note enclosed stating the reason or purpose. On the other hand, at the bottom of the check in the left-hand area for accounting, a scripture verse was written: "And all the believers met together constantly and shared everything with each other, selling their possessions, and dividing with those in need" (Acts 2:44-45). Our spiritual strengths and understanding were at a much higher level, no doubt, yet we were in our infantile stages in certain areas to comprehend such a gesture never experienced by us! As we were perplexed, we thought it best to consult our Bible study teachers of the church, so we rang them up. Their reasoning and spiritual guidance to us was that this check was given to us by this man, whom they knew, to help us find a home to own in the area where this church was. It would then bring us closer and help avoid the driving twenty-three miles each way each Sunday. It was also made known to us that this kind man, with his big heart, had at that time sold some prime real estate, and with the proceeds from that sale exercised God's desire that all those who trust Him care enough to share, as the verses above speak! This kind deed had no other motives, no strings attached, except that someone helped us to find a good, comfortable home near the church location. This check would then come in handy for the basic down payment toward the new home when we found one. The time and year was now 1980, when home ownership was hard, for interest rates on home loans were at their highest, around 9.5 percent. At the right time, as we pondered with the check in our hands, we were surprised once again: life's course moved along in an orderly way.

This new friend was also from the same church, and had been inspired by our faithfulness to be a part of this church, coming from a distance. He wanted to invest his time for us, as he was a professional in the home insurance business, and was in touch with many real estate agents in the normal course of his work at his office.

So together Minnie and I joined him and he took us to various areas until we came upon a quiet neighborhood called Powder Springs in

Rev. Paul Kumar

the northwest part of the city of Atlanta. There were a few completed homes, and they were all occupied. Among them there was one home, lonely in its framework, but soon to become a beautiful home. We climbed up to the floorboards and looked at the building design. It had three bedrooms, two full baths, a basement, and some acreage around the house. By definition it was a tri-level home. Somehow Minnie, my wife, who scrambled across the floorboards, very gently exclaimed, "It is for us!" Our church friend and I walked toward the end of the street, amid a deep wooded area yet to be developed, to a temporary trailer office that sat there. The builder was in that trailer, and we discussed this one lonesome house that was available, and its cost, the interest rates in effect at that time, and what down payment was required to buy a contract. The builder calmly replied that the down payment was $2,000 for that home, whose selling price from him was $49,000. We just did not believe what we had heard, and immediately volunteered to hand over that check we had received for $2,000 toward the down payment as a contract for our new home to own.

In every part of this venture, it was very obvious that no human effort played a role in the outcome of the conclusion of buying a new home. The entire course was initiated from God's direction toward His people, where God's love was genuinely shared and has proven to reach out to us in the form of friendships. Rich ingredients such as this make America the melting pot for millions of people who truly are privileged and blessed to be a part of this great nation, as ARE WE! "Do not fear, nor be afraid, have I not told you from that time and declared it? (Yes it is so true, for it began in our lives in 1970.) You are my witnesses, Is there a God besides me? Indeed there is no other rock; I know not one!" (Isaiah 44:8). Our refuge: we moved into our beautiful new home in July 1981. The church friend who gave a part of his own money, the one who gave his own time, led us to Powder Springs, Georgia, and at the time of signing our homeowners' deed with the attorneys, this insurance agent from the church also went forth to prepay a full year's worth of the homeowner's insurance costs, along with the fire hazard Insurance. With a heart that Christ in His love and goodness allowed us to call a home of our own, He opened the doors to a world of our own. Such a gift can testify for faith in us as a family, who dedicated that home then and now to God and God alone. What a change to life's course!

LIFE'S STABILITY WITH FAITH

NOW WHAT IS FAITH? It is the confident assurance that something we want is going to happen. It is the certainty that what we hope for is waiting for us, even though we cannot see it up ahead (Hebrews 11:1). Into a new home, a new neighborhood, a new city, a new job, and all that a family needs to have peace of mind is now ours to begin a stable, blessed Life. It has to begin with God, by faith, in each member of our family.

By faith by believing in God, we know that the world, and the stars, in fact all things were made at God's command and that they were all made from things that can't be seen. (Hebrews 11:3)

And those whose faith has made them good, in God's sight must live by faith, trusting Him in everything! Otherwise if they shrink back, God will have no pleasure in them. (Hebrews 10:38)

These truths helped us to lay our firm foundations for our faith in whom we believed for life; now it's a journey henceforth for stability. That is what is meant by the scriptures that say no mere man has ever seen, heard, nor even imagined what wonderful things God has ready for those who love the Lord (1 Corinthians 2:9). Thus far in our life's journey, from way out in the sultry, sweltering hot asphalt roads of Madras, now known as Chennai, southern India, to the beauty of the Blue Ridge Mountains of Hayesville, North Carolina, we are planted in the big city of Atlanta. We see densely populated neighborhoods with thousands of people scurrying to and fro in their luxury motor cars; we recognize Atlanta to be a great city in the South.

There is a world of difference, truly in its literal description, from the present and the past. The year was 1981 and our children were attending new schools, and Minnie, my beloved wife, with such stalwart devotion, love, and faithfulness with her redemption story, made it more worthwhile! Stability amid tugging forces all around for greed, wealth, and progress to higher standards of living could have deceived our thinking. With a stable airline career with United Airlines, we were to mould our lives in the best way that God would have desired, not as the world would want us to do. There is the truth, and to compare them, each of these is worlds apart. In reflection on the past to the present gave us renewed strength, as a family, with no next of kin around us, except for the devotion of people around us we called friends. It is that spirit of America, where strangers become friends and are like family. Such is the refreshing tie that binds us even today. We in our family were experiencing miracle after miracle; we were learning to love others as God would want us to do. We were learning to care and share with others as they had already done to us, expecting nothing in return. Once again, that is the spirit of America, where generosity knows no limitations.

Be full of love for others, following the example of Christ who loved you and gave himself to God, as a sacrifice, to take away you sins. "And God was pleased for Christ's love for you was like sweet perfume to Him. (Ephesians 5:2)

As loving parents, we cared for and loved our children. As they were growing, and during that time in growing, often they made many mistakes. We learned not to abandon them to their ways of wrongdoing but stood by them with parental love, pointing out the extent of their mistakes and their consequences.

Rev. Paul Kumar

We instructed them to avoid going down that destructive path again. We also realized that as parents, our words of advice were as precious as gems; often they fell wayward, with no true changes to show from them in return! Prayer truly becomes the open door, asking God's intervention and His healing touch for disturbed minds, anxious hearts, and restoration in the family. We all wanted to be of one accord in everything we did; again it never was the case.

It seemed that we were drifting along life's calm waters, stable as our children moved from elementary to middle to high school over the treacherous terrain in education with higher learning. All three children graduated high school and ventured into the world on their own. Now to the present: each child with his and her own family walks down memory lane and is inspired to know of their early childhood days and years. With so much to distract our grownup children now, some strong pillars of early wisdom remind them to cling to the faith that was instilled in them: faith in the home, faith taught, and faith parents practiced. To think of early discipline at home while growing up, now it is a reminder that each manages their own careers with honesty, truth, and fairness for Christ to oversee as their most important peer. Our children needed to understand that scripture truly motivates and convicts, and requires deep commitment to believe. "And I am sure that God who began the good work within you will keep right on helping you grow in His Grace, until His task within you is finally finished on that day when Jesus Christ returns" (Philippians 1:6). Truly such a promise from God leads to life stable in faith! Walking down memory lane with Minnie, I often pause, reminding myself of the present with thirty-seven years in the beauty of marriage, with faithfulness, true love, and dedicated living for each other, all interwoven and meshed together. Two persons as One!

That is how husbands should treat their wives, loving them as parts of themselves. So again I say, a man must love his wife as a part of himself, and the wife must see to it, that she deeply respects her husband, obeying, praising and honoring him. (Ephesians 5:33)

Celebrating life each day with faith in Christ is a very noteworthy reminder for us, and the world in its modern society that beckons us to celebrate life with the world in its ways, its deception to evil; its lack of faith and our walk with Christ makes our decisions so very misguided, with lying and cheating and everything else in between, even looking down on others who just don't seem to fit into our league of popularity, fame, and notoriety! Ugly prejudices surface, and I look back to the time in 1968 with my wife, Minnie, in her young life, in her home, with the rich settings, luxuries all around, yet starved for real love at the home. In spite of Mom, Dad, three brothers, and most of all, a dear twin sister, all learned and prosperous in business, they never allowed themselves to consider the world around them, beneath their white-washed bungalow's balconies: the poor; the homeless' the sick lying by the roadside along with the lepers; the starving children begging for food, some emptying the roadside dumpsters for pieces of bread or grains of half-eaten rice, to satisfy their days of starvation. Wisdom gained in the world, without God's hand, in faith, is futile, going no further than the "self"! Scripture says, "Stop fooling yourselves. If you count yourselves above average in intelligence, as judged by the world's standards, you had better put this all aside and be a fool, rather than let it hold you back from the true wisdom from God" (1 Corinthians 3:18). I admit that neither Minnie nor I as parents are perfect, free of mistakes, before God's eyes. Our times of chastening, reviewing our day-to-day actions, will speak of our imperfections, and that corrections are needed. We ought to rely upon God's plans and His unmerited favor upon us each day. The Bible calls this "GRACE"! God truly holds us within the boundaries of His grace daily!

Understanding our personal growth in the faith toward God the father, His son, Christ, God in His Holy Spirit, three persons in one, we look back the annals of our life from 1968. Our life steps to climb came purely from heaven's healing rain, to a family that was parched dry with nothing to hold on to with hope for the next day. <u>HEALING</u> for my beloved wife, Minnie, came from heaven, for on earth she lost everything most precious to anyone: family, her blood kin, just because she chose to fall in love, and to a Christian man. This loss was a heavy toll, the entire love of a family, yet did not surpass what God offered and still does: <u>HEALING</u> for me, a true devoted husband, to care and love a fragile, wounded heart, when my mother with deep-rooted faith spoke with much bitterness and judged her son's actions in loving this Hindu woman.

My mother vowed that my marriage to Minnie would not last more than three days, and heaven's healing rain has filled our life's bowl with the tie that binds, God's love, along with our human love as man and wife for over three decades and then some.

Hatred in human hearts festers like that of a cyst that bursts out with poisonous venom that infects the soul, destroying the ability to love even our very own as a family! God looks down upon all people differently. God spoke with deep concern to the man Saul, who turned his life of hatred for Christians, and made a complete turnaround to become the great apostle Paul. God said,

"Know but I am with you, that is all you need. My power shows up best in weak people." Paul then spoke, "Now I am glad to boast about how weak I am, I am glad to be a living demonstration of Christ's power, instead of showing off my own power and abilities. Since I know it is all for Christ's good, I am quite happy about the thorn in my flesh (our trials) about insults and hardships, persecutions, and difficulties, for when I am weak, then I am made strong, the less I have, the more I depend on Him!" (2 Corinthians 12:9-10)

In my household, truly our dependency is daily totally upon Jesus Christ, His leading of our lives, in the way heaven chooses it to be. "Because the Lord is my shepherd, I have everything I need" (Psalms 23:1). I am not perfect, nor is Minnie, and we stagger alone on the wayside of the world and its enticements. We stumble with our own actions, habits, and thoughts, all contrary to God's desires, and we are challenged in our faith because evil lurks close by! "There was a time, when I wouldn't admit what a sinner I was but my dishonesty made me miserable and filled my days with frustration" (Psalms 32:3).

God has unfailing watch over Minnie and I, our three children, and their families now, as they are parents, for we were thirsting once again for more of our spiritual growth, and God's hand was so ready to lift me up, wanting me to be a messenger of the Good News that many may know of the wonder-working power, the love and the hand of miracles in my life and that of my family!

I am truly grateful to God for choosing me fit to be one to talk about Him to people, helping me to be faithful and to serve Him. God began His work in me from that moment when I entered that large church that gave me strong meats in spiritual food to grow. The church helped me to learn scriptures, accept the truths of the Bible, divide the truths in the Gospels, and speak of Christ, who came into the world to save sinners like me. The apostle Paul once again spoke, "How true it is, and how I long, that everyone should know it, that Christ Jesus came into the world to save sinners and I was the greatest of them all" (1 Timothy 15).

The apostle Paul again spoke, "But God had mercy on me, so that Christ Jesus could use me as an example to show everyone, how patient He is, with even the worst sinners, so that others will realize that they too can have everlasting Life!" (1 Timothy 1:16). The world promotes division even in our churches today, and among our church leaders. Many church leaders dissuade honest, faithful witnesses for God's glory from talking about their own salvation or life's events that changed their lives forever in Christ Jesus. Worldly credentials are required to back up their testimonies, to be able to proclaim Christ openly amid God's people. Titles on paper as credentials, diplomas, and courses completed from theological schools with a classroom environment is acceptable for being eligible and qualified to appear before a group of people in the church these days. The apostle Paul burdened by a very young man, and Paul desired him to be a preacher, looking back to the wonderful ways of this young man's upbringing in the faith by his loving grandmother. This young man's name was Timothy. Paul wrote to young Timothy, "What I am eager for, is that all the Christians there will be filled with Love, that comes from pure hearts, and their minds

Rev. Paul Kumar

will be clean and their faith strong. But these teachers have missed this whole idea, and spend their time arguing and talking foolishness" (1 Timothy 1:5-6). Sadly such thinking has crept into the minds of our churches and their leaders, that the offices of them are the epitome of the faith and Christ Jesus becomes secondary. Once again the apostle Paul said to young Timothy, whose heart burned with the fire to be a preacher, a pastor, to serve people, "If you explain this to the others, you will be doing your duty as a worthy pastor, who is fed by faith, and by the true teaching you have followed" (1 Timothy 4:6). I consider the writings of the apostle Paul to Timothy to be sound and worthy, equipped to his calling to be a preacher, a pastor. It was a foreword for me to be submissive to God's direction, and trust in me to serve Him as a preacher. Servitude with all humility ought to be the main ingredient in any Christian's walk of life in true reflection of Christ's love and purpose, sharing it with everyone around me. My daily prayer, like that of the Psalmist King David, is "Create in me a clean heart, O God, and renew a steadfast spirit in me" (Psalms 51:10). This prayer ought to be sincere, asking God's help for purity within me, and faithfulness for serving Christ, who already has given much, on an old rugged cross, that I may be free! The intent of my heart is to grow in Christ daily, and have an impact and influence upon my beloved wife, Minnie, in her walk with Christ also, since 1975. Now, about influence upon my children, their lives, and their families now: My prayer equally is that Minnie and I will be the influence for our children to depend on for their lifetime with God, His son, Jesus Christ, and His Holy Spirit to guide them, and that they enjoy the joys of their salvation, that their walk with Christ be fresh and pure like that of a spring gushing forth always, and not a moment of rapture with gladness in their hearts.

God has truly been faithful in the lives of Paul and Minnie and their three children, Victor, Monisha, and Sabrina. "For thus says the Lord, the high and lofty one, who inhabits eternity, whose name is Holy, I dwell in the High and Holy place" (Isaiah 57:15). We are much blessed to dwell in this land, a land of plenty, America. God's instructions for our lifetime are as follows:

"And now, Israel, what does the Lord your God require of you, but to fear the Lord your God to walk in all His ways, and to love Him, to serve the Lord your God with all your heart and all your soul. And to keep the commandments of the Lord and to worship Him for your own good!" (Deuteronomy 10:12-13). Simple, basic expectations from me, as God does watch over me and my family. God's instructions help me build a stronger faith in Him, a total trust, and total reliance upon Him. This is in recognition of God's true love, mercy, and the unmerited favor upon me, and all who will believe, just as King David knew, "Your goodness and unfailing kindness shall be with me, all of my life, and afterwards I will live with you forever in your home" (Psalms 23:6). Life's fleeting moments will pass surely for everyone of us. Mortal death is sure. It is one of sadness and sorrow, yet I am ready to call heaven my eternal home; so is my beloved, when she is called, because of her faith so strong from idolatry to trust in a living Savior, her God, her maker, her sustainer, her refuge, her peace! What is your hope in life today?

Jesus Christ is the answer for such eternal hope, and that is more than enough to make many a tossed-about life to become one of stability ... "life's stability with faith."

In the words of a hymn written by Anna L. Waring in 1823, "In heavenly love abiding, no change my heart shall fear, and safe is such confiding, for nothing changes here. The storm may roar without me, my heart may low be laid, but God is round about me, and how can I be dismayed?"

> Would you truly understand the greatness of the love of our Savior Christ? Would you long to have Him round about you, near you, for He waits!

Rev. Paul Kumar

LIFE'S PURPOSE CONCLUSION

EVERY MORTAL BEING HAS A PURPOSE in life. It surely is a vital part of our living, to reflect, act upon, and go forward even into the unknown, with one sure, steady hand to hold on to. That is the very purpose in my writings: to help anyone, maybe you, envision how much more there is in life for us to accomplish if we trust and allow the Master, Christ, to hold our hands in His firm grip. With each of us, as humans, become aware, honestly, that there is God the father, His son, Jesus Christ, God in His Holy Spirit, three in one—the blessed Trinity—and believe, we must respond to that belief with unfailing devotion, and submit with humility that God in His heavenly grace and direction will be the mainstay for our lives and an ingredient to enhanced life, as God smiles upon us (YOU) calling us (YOU) His very own.

There is nothing extraordinary in me (Paul Kumar) nor in my wife Minnie (Menuka Kumar) to have been the recipients of such powerful words spoken up close and personal, from God's word, the Bible: "For I am God—I only—and there is no other like me, who can tell you what is going to happen. All I say will come to pass, for I do whatever I wish.

I have said I would do it, and I will" (Isaiah 46:9-11). The surrender of Minnie and I, much later in 1975, in tearful yet amazing reminiscences in the pages of this book, is written with the hope that for you it will not just end within the pages, but will inspire you, motivate you, to seek and find truth to embrace God's direction in your life, into the future, with a purpose for your life's purpose.

> And I am sure, that God who began the good work in you, will keep right on helping you grow, in His Grace, until His task within you is finally finished On that day when Jesus Christ returns.Phillippians 1:6

Rev.Paul Kumar.

Printed in the United States
122953LV00003B/541-549/A